— The —
WORLD
of **AFRICAN**
WILDLIFE

A safari guide for young explorers

Owen Hendry

Published by Struik Nature
(an imprint of Penguin Random House South Africa (Pty) Ltd)
Reg. No. 1953/000441/07
The Estuaries No. 4, Oxbow Crescent, Century Avenue, Century City, 7441
PO Box 1144, Cape Town, 8000 South Africa

Visit **www.struiknature.co.za** and join the
Struik Nature Club for updates, news, events and special offers.

First published in 2022
3 5 7 9 10 8 6 4

Copyright © in text, 2022: Penguin Random House South Africa (Pty) Ltd, Owen Hendry
Copyright © in photographs and illustrations, 2022: As credited on page 64
Copyright © in published edition, 2022: Penguin Random House South Africa (Pty) Ltd

Publisher: Pippa Parker
Managing editor: Roelien Theron
Editor: Heléne Booyens
Designer: Gillian Black
Picture researcher: Colette Stott
Proofreader: Helen de Villiers

Reproduction by Studio Repro
Printed and bound in China by Golden Prosperity Printing & Packaging (Heyuan) Co., Ltd

MIX
Paper | Supporting responsible forestry
FSC® C178225

Making illegal copies of this publication, distributing them unlawfully or sharing them on social media without the written permission of the publisher may lead to civil claims or criminal complaints. Protect the communities who are sustained by creativity.

All rights reserved. No part of this publication may be reproduced, stored in a retrieval system, or transmitted, in any form or by any means, electronic, mechanical, photocopying, recording or otherwise, without the prior written permission of the copyright owner(s).

ISBN 978 1 77584 805 9 (Print)
ISBN 978 1 77584 806 6 (ePub)

Also available in Afrikaans as
Die Wilde Wêreld van Afrika – 'n safari-gids vir jong verkenners
ISBN 978 177584 807 3

Contents

Introduction	4	Beating the heat	38
Meet the mammals	6	Family life	42
The Big 5	8	Nests & dens	46
Bountiful birds	12	At the water	48
Slithering & scuttling	16	Night life	52
Terrific trees	18	Scat facts	56
Survival in the wild	20	Tracks & signs	58
Finding food	24	Answers	62
On the hunt	28	Glossary	63
Around the kill	32	Picture credits	64
Courting & conflict	34		

INTRODUCTION
Africa

is home to some of the most interesting and diverse animals on Earth, from giant African elephants, barrel-shaped hippos and rotund rhinos to lanky giraffes, secretive aardvarks, menacing hyenas and striped zebras. Few places can compete with the variety and magnificence of wildlife found here.

Most of our wild animals are protected in game reserves. A visit to a game reserve is exciting, and a perfect opportunity to view and learn about all the many different kinds of creatures in their natural habitats, as they follow the rhythms of daily living.

GAME RESERVES IN AFRICA

KORUP
BOMA
AWASH
GARAMBA
MAIKO
LOPÉ
SALONGA
SERENGETI
UPEMBA
CAMEIA
W
KAFUE
ETOSHA
OKAVANGO SWAMPS
HWANGE
NAMIB NAUKLUFT
KGALAGADI
KRUGER
HLUHLUWE/MFOLOZI
ISIMANGALISO WETLAND PARK
KAROO
ADDO

WHAT IS WILDLIFE?

Wildlife includes creatures of all sizes and shapes: mammals, birds, reptiles, frogs, insects, and more ...

Life in the wild is about survival — finding food and water; coping with heat, drought and cold; escaping enemies; finding a mate; and raising young. It's always a struggle — and often dangerous.

Lioness mothers raise their cubs in a pride made up of several females and their young.

DO'S & DON'TS in the GAME RESERVE

DO
- ✔ Stay inside your vehicle unless signs permit otherwise.
- ✔ Return to camp before the gates close.
- ✔ Adhere to the speed limits.
- ✔ Keep your rubbish in your vehicle and dispose of it properly later.
- ✔ Keep still and quiet as you watch game.

DON'T
- ✗ Feed any animal or bird.
- ✗ Remove any plant or object.

DON'T be tempted to pick up a tortoise you see crossing a road. It may take fright and squirt liquid, losing valuable moisture it has stored for drier months.

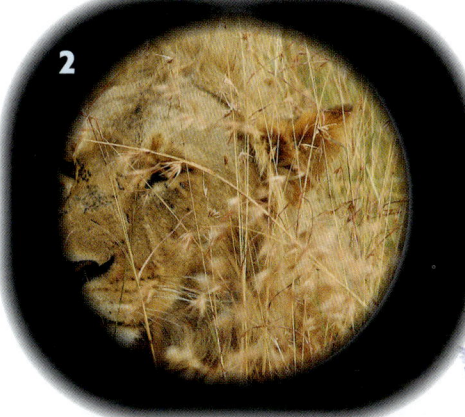

Spare us a Thought

Sharp sight

You need sharp eyes to spot certain animals in the game reserve. Some are plentiful and easy to see, but many animals remain hidden, and are much trickier to spot in the bush. The harder you look and the more patient you are, the more you will see.

You may catch only a glimpse of an animal. Can you guess what our young explorer sees through his binoculars?

5

Meet the MAMMALS

In Africa, mammals range in size from rodents, such as mice and moles, to the enormous elephant and hippopotamus. They include large carnivores or meat eaters such as lions, hyenas and wild dogs, plant eaters or herbivores — antelopes, rhinos, porcupines, warthogs and many others — and omnivores, which eat both plant and animal matter.

Large carnivores

These are the hunters of the wild, whose strategies for capturing prey differ from species to species. Some, such as lions and hyenas, work in groups to chase down prey, while the cheetah and leopard, among others, hunt alone. Carnivores use their highly developed senses of hearing, smell and eyesight to detect prey.

Carnivores are generally opportunists too, and will readily scavenge — eating prey that others have killed.

Small carnivores

Jackals, mongooses, small cats, otters, civets, genets, polecats and the termite-eating aardwolf are examples of smaller carnivores. Other than the mongooses, they are active at night when prey species such as rodents, insects and frogs are active too. Many also eat birds and their eggs.

The African wild cat is an adept hunter, especially of small rodents.

Leopards are carnivores that hunt alone.

Male lions on a kill

Wild dogs are meat eaters and work as a pack to hunt and kill their prey.

Existing on a diet of termites and other insects, aardwolves are carnivorous too.

Animal anagrams

Shuffle the letters to find the name of the mammal species.

1. preload
2. rephrasing
3. tab
4. asides
5. riffage
6. barged
7. evict
8. noli

On the wing

Bats are the only mammals that are able to fly. Their wings are made of skin stretched between their long, thin finger bones. Like other mammals, baby bats are born live (not from eggs), have fur, and suckle milk from their mother.

Herbivores

Plant-eating mammals are plentiful and varied, and often the easiest to see in the game reserve. Many become the prey animals of the large carnivores — and have developed special techniques to avoid being eaten (see p. 20). **Antelopes** are hooved animals varying in size from the massive eland to the tiny blue duiker. Some are *grazers*, feeding on grass, and some are *browsers*, eating leaves, soft shoots and shrubs. Kudus are browsers while wildebeest are grazers and impalas both graze and browse.

Giraffes are browsers whose long neck allows them to reach tender leaves that are beyond the reach of other animals. **Elephants** are also herbivores but have a varied diet that includes fruits, grasses, bark, roots and leaves.

Other commonly seen herbivores include zebras, warthogs, rhinos and buffaloes.

Omnivores

Omnivores include Africa's primates — the monkeys, baboons and bushbabies or galagos. Hedgehogs and squirrels are also omnivores.

Monkeys and baboons enjoy a wide range of plant and animal food. Bushbabies (see p. 53) are tree dwellers and eat tree resin, wild fruit, insects, and also birds and their eggs.

Smith's bush squirrel eating berries

Blue duikers eat fruit, leaves and flowers.

Hippos graze mostly at night, preferring shorter grasses.

Vervet monkeys eat a wide range of fruit, but also flowers, leaves, seeds and insects.

Among other mammals encountered in the wild are mice and rats, moles and bats, dassies, hares and shrews. These little creatures are important food for foxes and jackals, honey badgers, civets and small wild cats, as well as birds of prey.

The Big 5

Elephant *Buffalo* *Rhino* *Lion* *Leopard*

The Big 5 are the animals that big-game hunters used to regard as the most dangerous to hunt on foot. These days, they are the five big mammals that visitors to game reserves are most eager to see.

Rhino: Endangered giant

There are two rhino species in Africa: the black rhino and the white rhino. Both have been hunted for their horns and are now Endangered. The black rhino is not black, and the white rhino is not white — both are grey. Their names might have come about because the white rhino has a 'wide', square-lipped mouth, which became confused with 'white', so the other rhino was called 'black' simply because it was different.

Rhinos are huge — exceeded in weight only by elephants. Few predators risk attacking even young rhinos because of their size. Their biggest threat is humans. Poachers kill rhinos for their horns, which are ground up and used in traditional medicine by people who believe that the horns can cure illnesses.

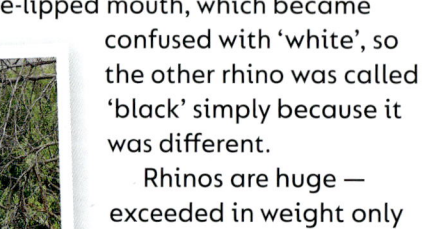

Rhinos are territorial. They mark their home ranges by dropping their dung in middens.

Black rhino

DID YOU KNOW? White rhino calves walk ahead of their mother, but black rhino calves follow behind. This is probably because black rhinos live in thicker bushveld than white rhinos, so the mothers need to clear a path for their infants.

White rhino mother and calf

A lioness with her cub

Lion: Top predator

Lions are the biggest of the carnivores. They have no natural enemies, and their main preoccupation is to find food. Lions hunt mainly at night. During the day, especially in hot weather, they find a shady spot under trees to rest and to keep cool. A sleeping lion uses less energy, so sleeping for up to sixteen hours a day is an important way to make a meal last for as long as possible.

DID YOU KNOW? A large mane is a sign that a male lion is healthy and strong, and a large, dark-coloured mane is even better. The mane is a warning to other males not to get into a fight. It also attracts female lions that are ready to mate, because a heavy-maned mate can be expected to produce strong, healthy cubs.

Word ladder

Change one letter at a time to make a new word that matches the clue. Can you reach the last word?

CLAW
CLAP = applaud
_ _ _ _ = wings do this
_ _ _ _ = total failure
_ _ _ _ = to move smoothly
_ _ _ _ = to shine in the dark
GROW

HORN
CORN = maize
_ _ _ _ = bottle stopper
_ _ _ _ = cutlery
_ _ _ _ = building for defence
_ _ _ _ = end of leg
ROOT

Elephant: Brainy and brawny

Elephants are among the most intelligent animals in the world. They have good memories and are able to learn too. They communicate using many different sounds that practically add up to being a language. Elephants are known to show compassion and grief when companions die.

The elephant's trunk is controlled by 50,000 different muscles. It is used for feeding and drinking, but also for smelling, feeling, trumpeting, caressing other elephants, lifting things and it is even used as a weapon. When crossing deep rivers, elephants use their trunk as a snorkel to enable them to breathe under water.

Big Cat Tracks

Lion

Cheetah

Leopard

Leopards are excellent climbers.

Leopard: Secretive hunter

If you are in a wild area at night and hear a coarse, rasping sound, almost like wood being sawed, this is the voice of the leopard, a solitary, shy carnivore that hunts in the hours of darkness.

When a leopard makes a kill, it will often drag the carcass into a tree for safekeeping, well out of the way of other predators. Adult leopards come together only to mate, and then part again after a few days. Only the female is responsible for protecting and bringing up the cubs.

DID YOU KNOW? When wounded, most animals run away and hide. However, when a leopard is wounded or cornered it becomes aggressive and will instinctively attack whatever has threatened it.

Mother leopard with her growing cubs

Who's who?

LEOPARD
- Heavy and powerful
- Spots grouped in rosettes
- Face heavily spotted

CHEETAH
- Slim, built for speed
- Marked with single spots
- Few spots on face; black 'tear' stripes from eyes

White rhino versus **Black rhino**

The white rhino has square-shaped lips, suited to grazing grass. The black rhino has a pointed or hooked upper lip, perfect for nipping twigs and leaves from bushes.

Buffalo: Strong and short-tempered

Big-game hunters in the past included the buffalo in their 'Big 5' because buffaloes killed more hunters than any other species did. They believed that a wounded buffalo would remember its attacker and seek him out to take revenge.

Should buffaloes notice a lurking predator, some of the herd will attack it and chase it away while others will cluster around the young animals to protect them.

Buffalo herds can be enormous, but on the move, they tend to spread out and it's not possible to see the size of the herd. If you stop to look at buffaloes alongside the road, you may suddenly find that your vehicle is surrounded by a massive, slow-moving herd hidden among trees and bushes. If this happens, be patient. Buffaloes have short tempers, and the worst thing drivers can do is to hoot or push their way through them. If the animals aren't disturbed, they will quietly walk round you, and you will have an amazing bushveld experience.

Buffalo herd

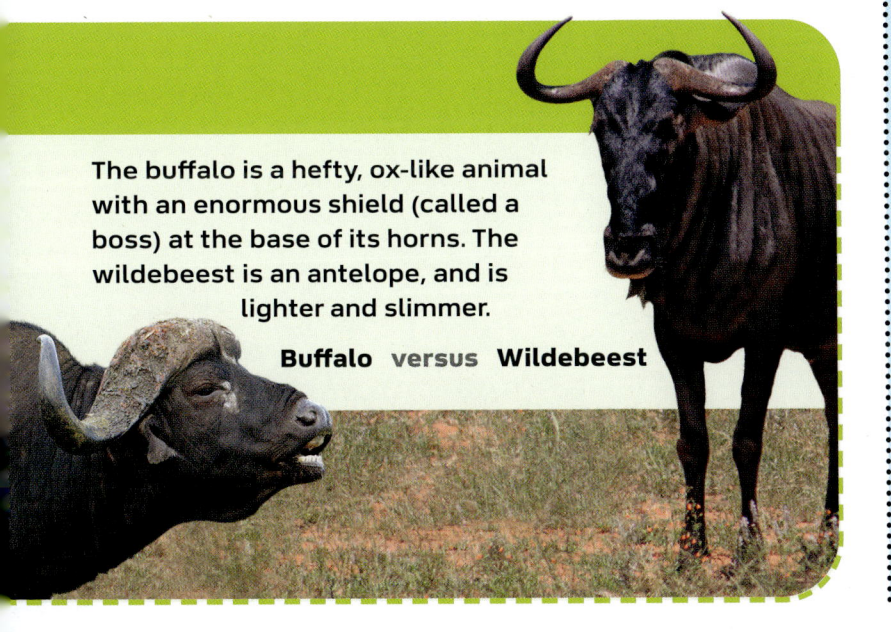

The buffalo is a hefty, ox-like animal with an enormous shield (called a boss) at the base of its horns. The wildebeest is an antelope, and is lighter and slimmer.

Buffalo versus Wildebeest

The Little Five

The Little Five remind us to look out for smaller creatures too. Their names link to the better-known Big 5.

The small, mouse-like **elephant shrew** is named for its long snout. It seldom comes out of the undergrowth, where it hunts for insects, spiders and worms. It sometimes eats seeds and small fruits.

Antlions are a group of insects that resemble dragonflies. They mostly fly at dusk and during the night. Read about the fierce larvae of these insects on p. 59.

Rhinoceros beetles are extremely strong for their size. If humans were as strong as these sturdy insects, we would be able to lift eight elephants. Only the males have horns, which they use to defend their territory.

The beautifully marked **leopard tortoise** can live to be 100 years old. It eats a variety of plants, and often gnaws on old bones to get the calcium its body needs.

Red-billed buffalo weavers live in large colonies. They eat insects, spiders and scorpions, as well as seeds and fruit.

BOUNTIFUL birds

Flight allows birds to move and live anywhere they choose, but birds are more varied and abundant in protected, unspoiled areas like game reserves because this is their natural home. Africa has more than 2,000 types or *species* of bird and southern Africa more than 900 species.

Fine feathers

Feathers are unique to birds and are important for more than just flying. They also
- protect birds against cold and heat
- provide waterproofing
- help some birds to blend with their surroundings and hide, through camouflage
- help some to be noticed: many males are brightly coloured

Rock pigeon

Great white pelican

Southern double-collared sunbird

Cape eagle-owl

Preening

Birds use their beak to tidy and clean their feathers. This helps to remove dirt and parasites.

Oil is produced by a gland near the base of the tail of most bird species. Preening helps to spread the oil over all the feathers and make them waterproof.

Lesser flamingoes inhabit salt pans, lagoons and estuaries.

BIRDS BY HABITAT

BIRDS in the AIR

Nearly all birds fly, but some spend *most* of their time in flight. These include swifts, swallows and martins. Although these birds look similar, there are ways of telling which is which.

SWIFTS
- appear all dark in flight
- aren't able to perch on wires or branches
- may cling to surfaces like buildings or cliff-faces
- have slender wings that sweep back
- have a tail that can be square or forked

SWALLOWS
- have mostly glossy-blue upperparts
- have white, rusty or streaked underparts
- are able to perch
- have wider, more rounded wings than swifts
- have a forked tail

MARTINS
- have a brownish body
- are paler underneath
- can perch
- have a mostly squarish tail

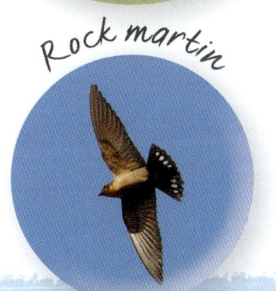

White-rumped swift

Red-breasted swallow

Rock martin

White-backed vulture

Birds of prey

Birds of prey are among the most spectacular of birds. Also known as raptors, these are the meat eaters that hunt and feed on small mammals, reptiles and other birds. They include eagles, hawks, vultures, falcons, harriers, buzzards and kestrels. Owls are also birds of prey, but unlike the others, they hunt at night.

BIRDS on the GROUND

Birds that are most often seen walking or pecking on the ground include francolins, sandgrouse, guineafowl, ostriches, cranes, bustards and korhaans, the secretary-bird and the large and boldly coloured ground hornbill.

Secretary-bird

BIRDS in and around WATER

Many birds spend their time in, on or around rivers and dams. They include ducks and geese, some kingfishers, flamingoes, herons, storks, jacanas, coots, crakes and moorhens. Large rivers also attract the remarkable African fish eagle, which swoops down from a high perch to catch fish.

Pied kingfisher

HOW TO IDENTIFY BIRDS

Start by learning the PARTS OF A BIRD so that you can easily note down obvious markings, colours and other features.

When you spot a bird, keep as still and quiet as possible so as not to scare it away.

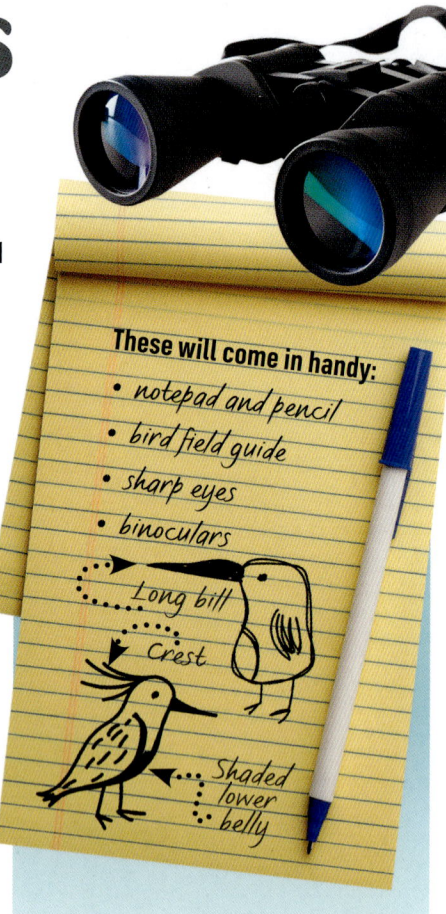

Labels on bird: crown, eye ring, forehead, beak, chin, throat, breast, belly, tibia, tarsus, toes, tail, rump, back, mantle, shoulder, nape

These will come in handy:
- notepad and pencil
- bird field guide
- sharp eyes
- binoculars

Long bill
Crest
Shaded lower belly

MAKE NOTES OF

- the general shape and size — think of a bird you know and decide whether the bird you see is bigger or smaller than it (See Jizz, opposite).
- any colours or markings and where they are (see labelled bird above for body parts).
- bill shape and feet.
- leg length and colour.
- tail length and shape.
- posture — is the bird upright or hunched?
- habitat — where is the bird?
  - in or near water?
  - in a tree?
  - probing on the ground?
  - walking in grass?

With these details jotted down, it will be easier to find the bird in a field guide.

BIRD FEATURES

SHAPE Francolins are round; egrets are slender.

POSTURE Lapwings stand upright, while sandgrouse are more horizontal.

TAILS The African darter has a long pointed tail; coucals have a broad tail.

BILLS The yellow-billed duck has a flattened bill; white-eyes have a small pointed bill.

COLOUR AND MARKINGS Colour is an important clue to identity — overall, as well as the 'flashes of colour' seen under the wing, on a shoulder or on the rump.

Sandgrouse have a horizontal posture.

The grey waxbill has a red rump.

Note the sharp pointed bill of this bee-eater.

Jizz

Jizz refers to the general shape and size of a bird without considering any details. Look at the silhouettes below and see if you can tell which group of birds each belongs to. This general shape is an important step in identification because once you can link the shape of the bird you saw to a particular group of birds, it is much easier to identify it using a field guide.

Match the silhouettes to the correct bird group:
1. owl
2. heron
3. dove
4. vulture
5. guineafowl
6. sunbird

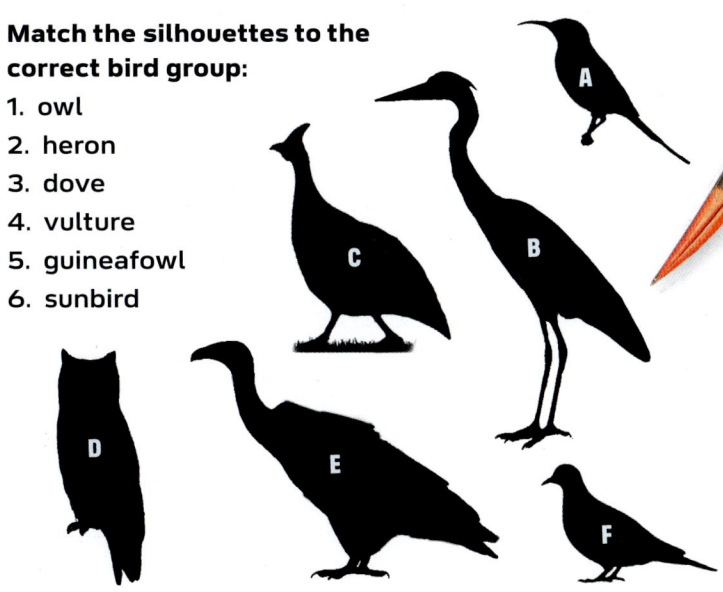

Word puzzle

Fit the words into the grid.

preen   vulture   wings
flamingo buzzard   parrot
jizz   crow   owls

G U I N E A F O W L

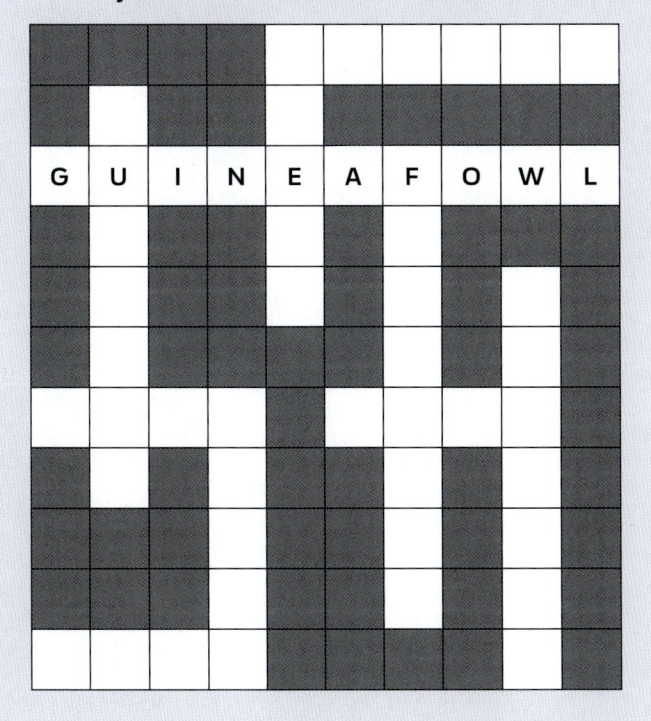

The Big SIX

The **martial eagle** is the biggest and most powerful of the African eagles.

Saddle-billed storks are boldly coloured. They are Endangered birds — their numbers are dwindling.

The **kori bustard** is the heaviest animal on Earth that's capable of flight.

The **ground hornbill** is the largest member of the hornbill family.

The **lappet-faced vulture** is the biggest African vulture.

Pel's fishing owl is the largest of Africa's owls.

15

Slithering & scuttling

A defensive cobra spreads its hood to appear larger and more threatening.

The natural world is full of creatures that seem creepy at first glance. Once you learn more about them, however, you'll understand why they look and behave the way they do, and the important role they play in nature.

Reptiles

Snakes, lizards, crocodiles, tortoises, turtles and terrapins are all reptiles. Of them, snakes probably have the scariest reputation. In reality, snakes are shy — when they see a possible threat (such as a human), their first instinct is to get away and hide. If they are taken by surprise or can't escape, they might try to scare off the intruder with a warning display: by rearing up and hissing, for example. If the threat continues to approach, only then will a snake strike. If you see a snake, immediately back off at least a few metres. Never pick up a snake (even if it looks dead), and don't walk in the bush barefoot or in sandals.

Mozambique spitting cobra

Namib gecko

Snake or skink?

It may look like a snake, but this slender reptile is actually a lizard — the nonvenomous Cape legless skink. It spends most of its time underground, using its snout to burrow through the soil as it hunts termites, larvae and earthworms. Legs are more of a hindrance than a help, so, over millions of years, this lizard has lost its limbs.

A rhombic egg-eater will hiss and strike when a human comes too close — but it's a bluff. It has almost no teeth and is harmless.

DID YOU KNOW? It's a myth that snakes are slimy. Their scales are actually cool and dry to the touch. As a snake grows, its skin does not. Instead, a new layer grows under the old one. The snake rubs its snout against a rock to tear the old outer layer, and squirms out of the old skin the same way you'd peel off a sock.

Know your scorpions

Scorpions, like spiders and mites, have eight legs. They have a pair of pincers at the front and a segmented tail with a sting at the tip. The thicker a scorpion's tail and the smaller its pincers, the more venomous its sting. Big, intimidating pincers mean that the venom is less potent. When visiting the bush, think twice before you overturn a rock. Be sure to check inside your shoes before putting them on — just in case a scorpion has mistaken them for a hiding place.

Thick tail = more potent venom

Big pincers = less potent venom

Thin pincers

Eight-legged allies

Spiders are a vital part of the wild. As predators, they keep insect populations in check. Without them, we would be overrun by mosquitoes, flies and other bothersome insects. All spiders produce silk. Some use it to capture prey, spinning sticky webs, building trapdoors or binding up victims. Others use silk to construct shelters or wrap their eggs.

Baboon spiders hide in silk-lined burrows, waiting to snatch unsuspecting prey.

Chasing shadows

Solifuges, or red romans, aren't true spiders. They don't produce silk or spin webs. These nocturnal creatures have a habit of seemingly 'chasing' people. They are, in fact, just trying to avoid the light by staying in the human's shadow.

Solifuge

Millipede

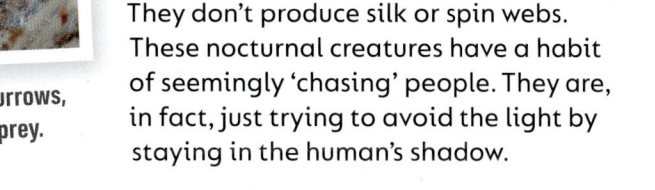

Bugs with benefits

Despite their small size, insects play a crucial role in nature. They pollinate flowering plants, disperse seeds, burrow through the topsoil, keeping it from becoming hard and compacted, and clean up detritus and dead bodies. They also serve as food for many creatures, such as insect-eating birds, reptiles and amphibians.

Millipedes are more closely related to lobsters than to insects! They have two pairs of legs on each body segment, and feed on dead or dying plants.

Terrific trees

Trees are among the most striking features of the African landscape. They are just as important as the wildlife because they provide shelter, protection, food and homes for many birds, insects, reptiles and mammals.

Umbrella thorn

The almost-flat-topped **umbrella thorn tree** is a common sight in the African bushveld and grasslands. Its trunk divides into many branches, topped by a leafy, umbrella-shaped canopy. Antelopes, monkeys and giraffes eat its leaves and tightly curled seed pods, and elephants feast on the bark of mature trees.

The umbrella thorn is armed with both straight and hooked thorns that easily catch on fur and clothing, giving it its Afrikaans name, 'haak-en-steek bos'.

Seed pods

DID YOU KNOW? The gum of the umbrella thorn, which is rich in carbohydrates, is eaten by lesser bushbabies, vervet monkeys and baboons.

Baobab

Baobabs are distinctively African trees and live longer and grow larger than any other plants in Africa. For most of the year, baobabs have no leaves and seem to be growing upside down, the branches looking like roots reaching for the sky.

Baobab seeds provide a tasty snack for monkeys, while elephants enjoy the nutritious bark, bushbabies eat the fruit, and fruit bats feed on the sweet flower nectar.

The trees have all sorts of uses for humans too: young leaves are cooked as a vegetable; rope and baskets are made from the bark fibres; and seeds can be roasted to make a type of coffee.

Baobab tree

Baobab fruit

Baobabs bear leaves for just three or four months each year.

Fever tree bark

FEVER TREE: Early explorers to Africa noticed that when they camped in swampy areas and close to rivers where these greeny-yellow-barked trees grew, they would get sick with malaria. They blamed the trees and so named them 'fever trees'. Scientists then discovered that malaria was spread not by the trees, but by the mosquitoes that lived in the same damp regions. But the name stuck! Elephants enjoy eating the bark of these unusual trees.

Marula fruit

The **marula tree** is topped by a rounded canopy that is easily spotted throughout the bushveld. In late summer female trees produce plum-sized fruits that drop to the ground while still green. Once ripe, they provide a juicy treat for monkeys, baboons, zebras, elephants and many species of antelope. The fruit is also used to make jam, beer and liqueurs.

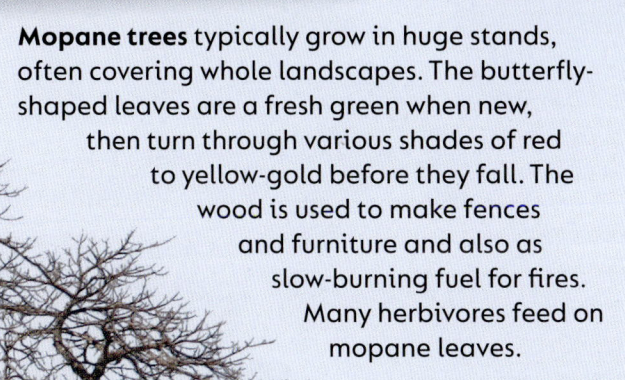

Mopane trees typically grow in huge stands, often covering whole landscapes. The butterfly-shaped leaves are a fresh green when new, then turn through various shades of red to yellow-gold before they fall. The wood is used to make fences and furniture and also as slow-burning fuel for fires. Many herbivores feed on mopane leaves.

Mopane leaves

Mopane worms feed on the leaves. The worms are dried and eaten by local people.

The **sausage tree** is another special African tree. Its fruits look just like large sausages, and hang from the tree all year round. Ripe fruit is enjoyed by monkeys and baboons, bushpigs, elephants, hippos and porcupines. Large red flowers that appear in spring are eaten by antelopes, and are visited by feeding insects, birds and bats.

Fruit of the sausage tree

Quiver tree

This large succulent tree grows only in the driest parts of southern Africa. In the past, San hunters would hollow out the branches to make quivers for their arrows. Many birds, insects and even baboons are attracted to the sweet nectar of the massed yellow flowers.

Survival in the wild

Almost all animals run the risk of being eaten. Their struggle to stay alive depends on various defence strategies that range from camouflage, warning coloration and special armour to using hooves and horns to fight or defend themselves.

Zebras' stripes are a form of defence. When the herd clusters together, predators have trouble picking out a single target to hunt, as it's hard to see where one zebra ends and the next begins.

Born to run

The babies of **zebras**, **wildebeest** and some other **antelopes** can stand up within minutes of being born. A wildebeest calf, for example, can run next to its mother within five minutes of its birth. Since herds travel far to find water and fresh grass, calves need to be mobile very quickly, otherwise they'll be picked off by predators. Many antelope species rely on speed to escape predators, and some can outrun lions and hyenas. The fastest African antelope is the **tsessebe**. It can run at speed for long distances — even the famously fast cheetah can't sprint for more than a minute.

Tsessebe calves are able to walk and run within an hour of being born.

A suricate sentry keeps an eye out for predators while the rest of the group relaxes.

Sound the alarm

Suricates, or meerkats, work as a team to stay safe from snakes, eagles, jackals and other carnivores. While some relax, play or forage for food, others take up sentry posts and keep watch. The sentries perch on their hind legs from high-up points, and chatter and squeal to communicate with the group. They use different calls to signal 'attacker from the sky', 'danger on the ground' and 'all clear'. These feisty animals will confront an attacker by crowding together and rushing forwards in a tight, noisy group that looks like one huge furry animal.

Food or foe?

A suricate scans its surroundings. Which of these would make it raise the alarm, telling its family of the danger?

A   B   C   D   E

These alert impalas have spotted a predator. They're safe as long as they can see it, since the predator has little chance of a kill without the element of surprise.

Safety in numbers

Many prey animals, such as **impalas** and **buffaloes**, live in large groups. With so many eyes, ears and noses sensing possible danger, it's hard for carnivores to sneak up unnoticed.

Large herds provide protection for the old, young and weak. When a buffalo herd is threatened, the healthy members of the group will encircle the weaker ones and point their deadly horns towards the attackers. Walking in long lines through the bush also offers some protection for large groups. It's quieter when moving like this, and if a predator appears, the animals can more easily scatter and escape.

Mimics and deceivers

Look closely at the plants and earth around you — some insects look just like grasses, leaves, twigs or pebbles to avoid being noticed. This form of disguise is called 'mimicry'. The **pearl-spotted owlet** employs a different method to bluff its raptor enemies. It has false eyes on the back of its head to make predators think they are being watched.

A moth bug mimics a leaf.

Stick insects look just like twigs, tricking predators so as not to be eaten.

Pearl-spotted owlet

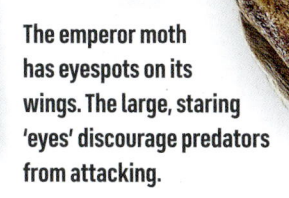

The emperor moth has eyespots on its wings. The large, staring 'eyes' discourage predators from attacking.

CLEVER CAMOUFLAGE

Prey animals rely on camouflage to conceal themselves, while predators use it to sneak closer. In **cryptic coloration**, the colour, patterning or shape of an animal helps it to blend in with its surroundings. In **disruptive coloration**, features such as blotches, stripes or spots break up the animal's outline, making it difficult for a predator to recognise it.

Can you detect the creatures below?

DID YOU KNOW? After giving birth, many antelope mothers hide their calves in thick bush, visiting them a few times a day to nurse. Calves are lightly coloured, which helps them blend in with grass and bushes. At this age the calves have no odour, and so don't attract the attention of predators.

21

Armoured animals

The **pangolin** is a remarkable animal. Its sticky tongue, used to lick up ants, is longer than its body, and its head, back and tail are covered in hard scales. The scales are made of keratin — the same material that makes hair, human fingernails, and the rhino's horn. The tail has scales with sharp edges, and can be used as a weapon to hit an attacker.

A pangolin will freeze at the smallest sign of danger, making it difficult to spot. When threatened, it rolls itself up into a tight ball, using its tail to cover its head and stomach. A mother pangolin will roll up around her baby to shield it.

DID YOU KNOW? Pangolins are more under threat from human poachers than they are from leopards, lions and other predators. They are hunted for bushmeat and for traditional medicines, and are traded more than any other animal in the world.

A pangolin rolls into a hard, spiky ball that is difficult for predators to bite through.

Spiky self-defence

Porcupines are protected by an armoury of spines and quills. The quills at the end of the tail are hollow, and make a rattling noise when shaken. When a porcupine is threatened, it will erect its quills to make itself look bigger, and shake its tail as a warning sign. If the danger continues, it will rush backwards or sideways at the attacker to drive its quills into it. The quills are loosely attached to the porcupine's body and are easily dislodged. Quills can cause severe wounds, which quickly become septic.

This lion tangled with a porcupine.

Warning signs

In nature, colour sometimes acts as a warning. For example, the poisonous **banded rubber frog** has bold orange-red stripes running along its black back. These 'warning colours' proclaim: 'Don't eat me — I'm poisonous'.

When threatened, the **striped polecat** lifts its tail and squirts a vile-smelling liquid at its enemy. Its vivid black-and-white-striped fur says: 'Don't disturb me — I smell too bad for you to eat me, and the liquid I squirt will irritate your eyes and nose'. Likewise, **honey badgers** are boldly marked in contrasting black-and-white colours to warn that they are ferocious fighters.

Banded rubber frogs are boldly coloured — a warning to other animals not to eat them.

A kick from a giraffe's hooves can smash a hyena's jaw.

Smaller drongos mob a kite to chase it away from their nest.

Fierce fighters

Carnivores risk serious injury, and even death, when they go in for a kill, since prey animals often fight back with teeth, hooves, horns and other weapons. Zebra stallions protect the herd and ward off attackers by kicking and biting them. Elephants are equally protective when defending their calves. Adult elephants swing their trunk, slash with their tusks and will even trample an attacker to defend a calf. Hippos use their tusks and sheer size as weapons of defence and attack. It would take a desperate predator to clash with a hippo.

Equipped with rapier-like horns, this gemsbok mother can easily defend her calf.

Who's mobbing who?

Mobbing happens when a few birds join together to chase a predator away. One bird signals to the other birds, then they all fly aggressively at the intruder, making a lot of noise while dive-bombing it.

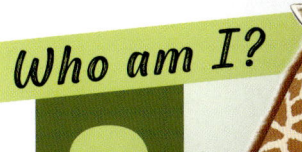

Who am I?

1. My thick dewlap protects me from predators aiming for the throat.
2. At a waterhole I make sure there are no predators nearby, because once I bend down to drink, I can't defend myself against an attacker or run away.
3. The pattern on my hide makes it difficult for a predator to pick me out from the herd.
4. The thick, loose skin around my neck protects me from bites, and allows me to twist around and defend myself ferociously.
5. I may not look it, but I am the fastest antelope in Africa.
6. I hop, jump, and sidestep like the very best rugby players.

Giraffe
Springbok
Eland
Tsessebe
Zebra
Honey badger

Finding food

Eating is essential for survival, so finding food is a key part of life in the wild. Many animals, especially herbivores, spend more time searching for food than doing anything else. There's much variety in the food that sustains wild animals and as many different ways of obtaining it.

Thorny problem

Giraffes eat the leaves, flowers and fruits of many tall trees, but their favourite trees are acacias, all of which have thorns or spikes. The giraffe uses its long tongue to carefully remove leaves from among the thorns. It also uses its teeth, tough lips and the hard roof of its mouth to strip off the leaves without being harmed by the thorns. It spits out any large thorns that are pulled off accidently.

DID YOU KNOW? Giraffes get the extra minerals they need by eating soil, and by chewing the bones of dead animals.

A long neck enables the giraffe to reach the fresh new growth at the tops of trees.

African elephant

Big meals

Elephants eat a huge amount of food. Each day they consume 150kg of grass, leaves, fruit, seeds and woody branches. Broken branches lying on the road are a sure sign that elephants have been in the area. They often push over small trees to reach the young leaves at the top, and pull up roots with their tusks. The damage caused is not always a bad thing. Elephants help to keep grasslands and savanna open. Without them, bushes and trees would take over and grass-eating animals would go hungry or move away.

DID YOU KNOW? Elephants can drink over a hundred litres of water a day. If they can't find surface water, they dig in river beds to reach underground water.

Bushbuck are solitary and guard their limited food supply by scent-marking their territory.

Chewing the cud

Ruminants are animals that re-chew their food to get as much nutrition from it as possible. Food is first mashed and ground in the mouth before it is passed into the rumen — a special chamber in the stomach. From here, coarse pieces of partially digested food are pushed back into the mouth to be chewed again. You might see an antelope slowly chomping, sometimes for hours, and often while lying down. This is known as 'chewing the cud'.

Roan antelope

Green living

Herbivores that are largely solitary, such as steenbok, bushbuck and duikers, live in relatively small territories, about the size of a few neighbourhood blocks. Their access to food is limited to these home ranges so they scent-mark the borders to keep other animals out. By contrast, large herds of grazing animals, like buffaloes, wildebeest and zebras, are always on the move, crossing vast distances in search of fresh new grass. Their home ranges can easily be as big as 1,000 square kilometres — bigger than some of the world's largest cities.

Kudu are browsers, and eat a wide range of woody and leafy plants.

Wildebeest herds move as the seasons change, covering enormous areas in their search for food and water. They often follow lightning and thunder to move towards distant rainfall, which promises greener pastures.

Upper tusks – blunt but effective

Lower tusks – sharp and dangerous

Bending to eat

Warthogs have a short neck and fairly long legs, so they often bend down or 'kneel' to graze or dig up roots and bulbs with their hard snouts. Special pads on their wrists protect them from injury while they shuffle along the ground. While they mostly feed on grass, they also eat fruit and bark, and occasionally small rodents, frogs and reptiles.

Warthogs have two pairs of tusks. They are used as weapons of defence and by males fighting for breeding rights.

Special pads on their wrists enable warthogs to 'kneel' when grazing.

Devouring dung

Many animals eat dung, but they do it for different reasons. Dung often contains undigested food fragments that are full of nutrients. **Rabbits**, **hares** and **hedgehogs** eat their own droppings for extra nutrition. Young **elephants**, **zebras**, **hippos** and **warthogs** eat the droppings of adults. These provide bacteria for their immature stomachs to help them digest the grass and plant material they eat. A **steenbok** mother eats the droppings of her lamb to keep the area free of any scent that might be picked up by a predator.

A baboon scratches in elephant dung for undigested seeds or fruit.

Dung maze

Dung beetles feed on droppings, sucking the smelly liquid from fresh poo. Navigate the maze to get the beetle to its meal.

DID YOU KNOW? Salt licks (or mineral licks) are natural places on the ground where there is a high concentration of salt and minerals. Animals lick the surface to absorb these minerals. In some game reserves rangers provide special salt licks to give animals access to mineral salts that may be absent from their diets.

Impalas gather around a specially placed salt lick for the mineral salts that are absent from the grass they eat.

Beaks and bills

The shape and size of a bird's beak can tell you a lot about what it eats.

Seed eaters
Sturdy, short and thick for cracking open hard seeds.

Insect eaters
Slender and pointed to snatch up insects and to probe into tree bark.

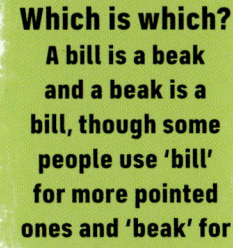

Meat eaters
Strong, sharp and hooked for tearing off meat.

Fish eaters
Spear-like, long and pointed to stab fish prey.

Fruit eaters
Hooked for tearing into fruit.

Nectar feeders
Long, thin and curved to reach into flowers for sweet nectar.

Bill or beak?

Which is which? A bill is a beak and a beak is a bill, though some people use 'bill' for more pointed ones and 'beak' for flatter ones.

Give and take

Some animals (and plants too) have evolved ways of working together so that both benefit. This type of relationship is called 'mutualism'. **Yellow-billed oxpeckers**, for example, help buffaloes, giraffes and hippos by removing ticks and flies from their skin. The birds are guaranteed a regular supply of food and the herbivores get free pest control.

Bees, butterflies and some birds have a similar relationship with flowers. The insects and birds fly from flower to flower to feed on nectar and pollen. When they visit a flower for food, pollen collects on their bodies and is then carried to other plants. In this way the flowers are pollinated, allowing them to produce seeds.

Oxpeckers search for ticks on a buffalo's face.

A monkey beetle feeds on wildflower pollen. While moving from plant to plant, it spreads the pollen.

Tagging along

Some birds and beasts have a one-way relationship, with one species benefiting while the other remains unaffected by it. The **cattle egret** is one such winner. These birds follow grazing antelopes, rhinos and buffaloes, and quickly seize the grasshoppers and other insects that leap out of the way of the large mammals.

Egrets with an impala

Missing letters

Fill in the vowels of special words that appear in this section.
1. c_d
2. t_ng_ _
3. br_ws_
4. t_sk
5. m_t_ _l_sm

On the hunt

Carnivores work hard to find food. They need to spot potential prey, sneak up close enough to strike, and chase the victim down as it tries to escape. They also risk being injured by animals that fight back. Hunting requires stealth, strategy and strength.

Lions are social animals, and live in prides. They work as a team to take down large prey, like this buffalo.

Pack tactics

Lions are heavy, extremely powerful, and fast over short distances. Although both male and female lions are good hunters, most of the hunting is done by the females. They are smaller and more agile, and can hide more easily than the males. A male lion may sometimes approach a herd of antelopes from upwind, so that the prey herd can smell it. The lion will then charge, panicking the herd and chasing it towards the female lions waiting undercover downwind.

Spotted hyenas are well known for scavenging. But they are skilled pack hunters too, and can bring down big prey, like this kudu.

African wild dog

Teamwork and endurance

African wild dogs (also known as painted wolves) are beautifully marked hunters that live in large packs. They are not as fast as other large carnivores, but can chase their prey for long distances without tiring and are very efficient hunters. They work as a team, chasing the prey until it tires and then attacking it to bring it down.

DID YOU KNOW? African wild dogs vote with their noses. When the pack must decide whether it's time to hunt, members that are willing and ready will start sneezing. The more sneezes, the more likely the pack will go out to hunt.

Word search

? How many hunting-related words can you find?

- PACK
- CHASE
- PREY
- PREDATOR
- RAPTOR
- TALON
- FANG
- CLAW
- POUNCE
- HUNT
- SPEED
- STALK
- DEATH
- TRACK

A	T	R	S	P	E	E	D	P	R	O	P	A	C	K
C	L	A	W	I	F	E	D	O	P	R	E	Y	T	P
O	S	P	C	H	A	S	E	U	D	A	T	P	A	R
L	T	T	P	R	N	C	A	N	S	P	R	Y	L	H
R	A	O	O	C	G	R	T	C	A	T	A	M	O	U
Y	L	R	F	F	O	T	H	E	C	O	C	L	N	N
P	K	X	P	R	E	D	A	T	O	R	K	I	L	T

The cheetah's long, heavy tail helps it balance and steer in a high-speed chase.

Built for speed

The **cheetah** is a slim, athletic cat with long legs and a small head. It is the fastest land animal in the world, and can reach a speed of over 100 km/h in just three seconds — accelerating faster than a Lamborghini. Sprinting at such a speed uses a lot of energy, so a chase is usually limited to a few hundred metres. After the tremendous effort of a high-speed chase, a cheetah can take half an hour to catch its breath and lower its heart rate. The cheetah may be fast, but it isn't powerful. With its small jaws and teeth, it is not able to overpower its prey and kill it with a single bite to the neck, as lions and leopards do. Instead, it brings its prey down by tripping it, then slowly strangles it with a sustained bite to the neck.

DID YOU KNOW? The peregrine falcon is the world's fastest living creature. It can move more than twice as fast as the cheetah. It preys mainly on other birds, grabbing them in mid-air.

Sharp senses

Eagles have excellent eyesight that enables them to find and catch prey. In daylight, an eagle can spot the movement of a hare more than three kilometres away.

Tawny eagle

The caracal has excellent hearing, improved by the hairy tufts that funnel sounds into its ears. This sturdy cat seeks out small prey animals to pounce on, and can leap high to take low-flying birds.

The clawless otter finds food by means of touch. With its sensitive fingers, it feels among the reeds, rocks and mud for molluscs, crabs and frogs.

Snakes smell the air using their tongue. The forked tongue is very sensitive and can easily track a victim's movements.

Mozambique spitting cobra

Little hunters

These four little mammals are skilled hunters. Can you match their descriptions to their names?

1. I have a very bushy tail. Outside game reserves farmers have mixed feelings about me, because although I help keep rodent numbers low, I can't resist stealing the chickens.
2. My face markings make it look as if I have a dark mask over my eyes.
3. I'm related to the mongoose family. I can become quite tame, and have been seen at bush camps boldly looking for food at meal times.
4. I look like a large tabby cat, and hunt by stalking and pouncing, catching prey with my front feet.

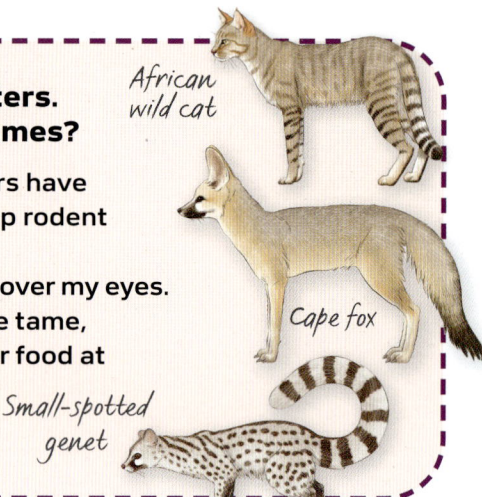

African civet

African wild cat

Cape fox

Small-spotted genet

Small but deadly

The **black-footed cat** is the smallest wild cat species in Africa — and one of the deadliest. Rats, mice and shrews are its favourite prey. It also catches rabbits and hares, and with a high pouncing leap can take small birds, both on the ground and in low flight. The tiny feline makes 10 to 14 kills each night. It is successful in 60% of its hunting attempts — a leopard, by contrast, has a 20% success rate.

Black-footed cat

The serval stalks its prey and finishes the hunt with a great leap.

Prehistoric predator

Crocodiles have hardly changed for 250 million years, and are among the most successful species ever. The Nile crocodile will lie motionless in the water waiting for the right moment to surprise its prey. Often just its eyes and nostrils are visible above the water. This huge reptile has the strongest bite in the animal kingdom. When it has bitten into a victim, it is impossible to force the jaws open. It drags the prey into deep water, and rolls violently. The 'death roll' helps to break the carcass into smaller pieces that the crocodile can swallow.

Nile crocodile

DID YOU KNOW? A crocodile produces strong stomach acid that dissolves not just meat but even hooves and horns. This reptile doesn't eat very often: an adult crocodile needs a good meal only once every few weeks.

Odd one out

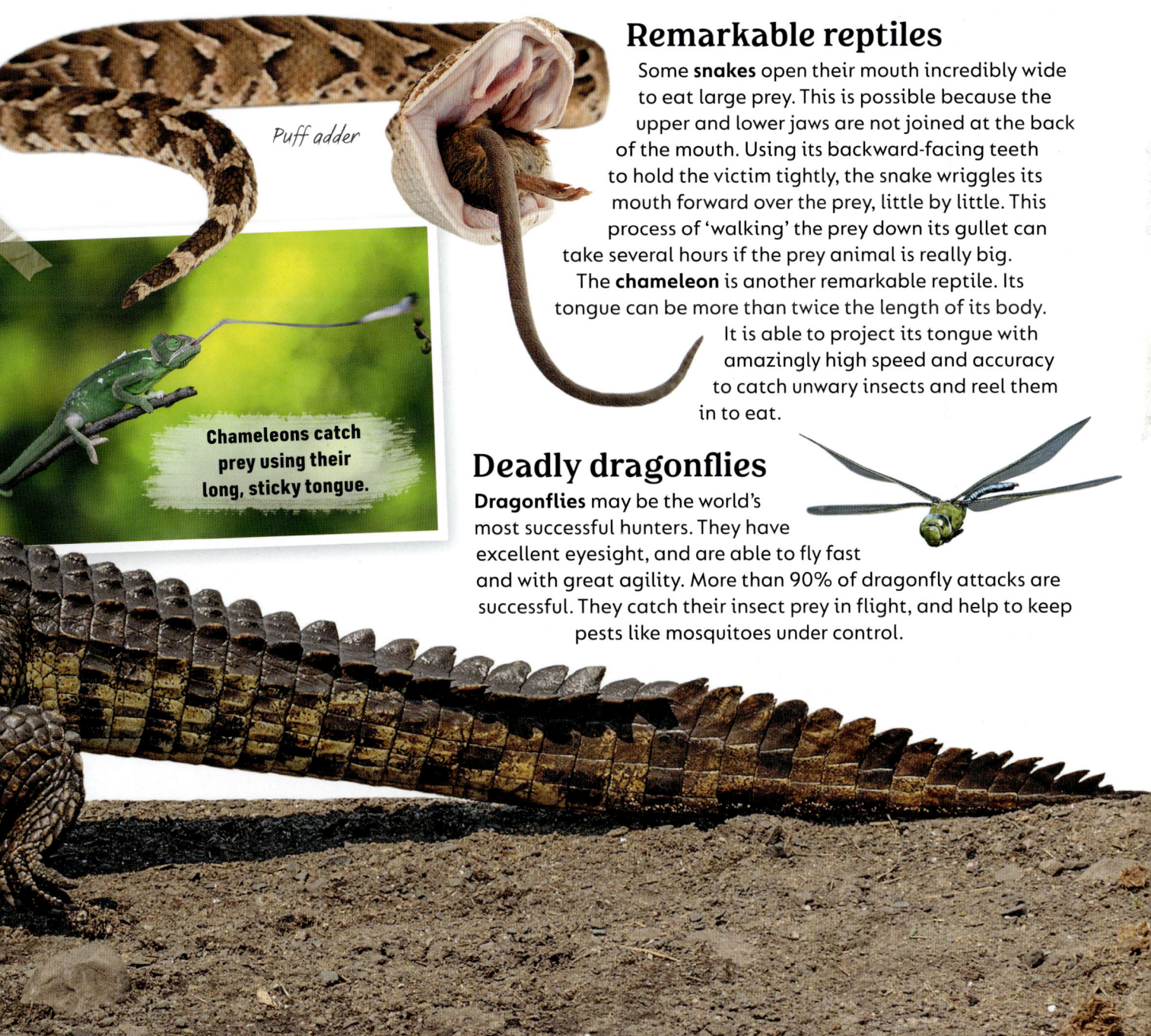

Birds that can seize, carry and kill their prey with their talons (claws) are called raptors. Which one of these carnivorous birds is not a raptor?

Bateleur eagles are the acrobats of the air, and are often seen soaring in search of prey.

Barn owl

Darter

Jackal buzzard

African harrier-hawk

Remarkable reptiles

Some **snakes** open their mouth incredibly wide to eat large prey. This is possible because the upper and lower jaws are not joined at the back of the mouth. Using its backward-facing teeth to hold the victim tightly, the snake wriggles its mouth forward over the prey, little by little. This process of 'walking' the prey down its gullet can take several hours if the prey animal is really big.

The **chameleon** is another remarkable reptile. Its tongue can be more than twice the length of its body. It is able to project its tongue with amazingly high speed and accuracy to catch unwary insects and reel them in to eat.

Puff adder

Chameleons catch prey using their long, sticky tongue.

Deadly dragonflies

Dragonflies may be the world's most successful hunters. They have excellent eyesight, and are able to fly fast and with great agility. More than 90% of dragonfly attacks are successful. They catch their insect prey in flight, and help to keep pests like mosquitoes under control.

Around the kill

Large carnivores rarely eat in peace. Other hungry meat eaters soon smell a kill and arrive to try and steal it. Vultures and other cunning scavengers, such as spotted hyenas, move in to claim their share. Jackals, foxes, marabou storks and crows follow. Beetles, flies and ants clean up the remains.

Who feeds first?

When a pride of **lions** makes a kill, the big males feed first, even if the females did the hunting. What remains is quickly eaten by the rest of the pride, who squabble over the leftovers. The cubs feed last and often go hungry if there is not enough food to go around.

African wild dogs work closely together in a pack to hunt down their prey, usually killing it by slicing through the hide and ripping the flesh apart. The pack feeds quietly, and there is no quarrelling at the scene. Bigger pups are given the option to feed first.

Lions won't willingly abandon a carcass until it's completely stripped.

Conflict at the carcass

Many large carnivores, including lions, will scavenge and steal kills when they can. So, when a predator makes a kill, it has three options: eat fast before the meal is stolen, hide the body, or defend the carcass against thieves. The **cheetah**, being smaller and less powerful than other big cats, won't risk getting injured defending a kill. Its strategy is to eat as much as it can as fast as possible, before it is chased away by lions, leopards and hyenas.

Cheetahs eat quickly, before other predators arrive to steal their kill.

Lappet-faced vulture

Spotted hyena

Black-backed jackal

Lookalikes

The **SPOTTED HYENA** has sloping shoulders, short back legs, and spotted fur. It is both a hunter and a scavenger, and has the strongest jaws of all the mammal predators, crushing bones to get at the nutritious marrow inside.

The **BROWN HYENA** has long dark hair, stripes on its legs, and pointed ears. It has an exceptional sense of smell and relies more on scavenging than on hunting, competing aggressively for the kills of other carnivores.

The **AARDWOLF** belongs to the same family as the hyenas but is smaller. It has a striped body and a bushy tail. It feeds almost exclusively on termites, which it licks off the soil surface with its long tongue.

A black-backed jackal, spotted hyena and lappet-faced vulture compete for a kill.

Cape vulture

Scavengers from the sky

Vultures are nature's clean-up crew, stripping the flesh off carcasses that would spread disease if left to rot. These birds have a strong digestive system and can eat carrion that would be harmful to other scavengers. Vultures like to wash at a waterhole or river after the messy business of feeding on a bloody carcass. Their head and neck are bare, making them easier to keep clean than if they were feathered.

DID YOU KNOW? The Lappet-faced vulture is a large and powerful scavenging bird. On warm days it soars high on thermals of rising warm air, scanning the ground for fresh kills. Its massive beak can tear through tough skin, ligaments and tendons that other birds can't process.

Squabbling for scraps

It is common to see an assortment of scavengers around a kill, all competing for a meal. Keep an eye out for the **marabou storks**. Their long, straight bill is better suited to catching reptiles, fish and frogs than to shearing meat. But they trail the other scavengers, ready to snatch any scraps that these animals may drop. **Black-backed jackals** are also quick to sniff out a kill, and wait for their chance to grab a morsel. The gathering gradually disperses once all the food has been taken.

Marabou stork

Courting & conflict

Gemsbok males fight to protect their territories and for the right to mate with females in a herd.

Courtship takes place when adult males want to attract female mates. It can involve elaborate dances and displays by both males and females as they communicate their interest in each other. Male animals often fight to show their strength and to win a female. Some male birds grow bright and beautiful plumage during the breeding season, tempting the females to choose them.

Fighting for rights

Equipped with fearsome weapons — horns, hooves and teeth — male antelopes challenge one another for the right to mate with females in a herd. During these displays of strength, each shoves and threatens the other until one finally retreats, defeated. Occasionally the fights become more than just noise and threats, and one of the contestants is badly wounded or even killed.

Normally solitary, leopards come together only when breeding.

DID YOU KNOW? Male giraffes 'neck-wrestle' for mating rights by hitting each other with their long necks; they sometimes also fight using their horns. The battle usually ends when one of the males is too tired to continue.

Courting males and females use their necks in a gentler way, rubbing them together as a show of affection.

Giraffe horns are called ossicones.

Courting cranes

Before mating, cranes perform a special kind of courting ritual. They first call to one another, then they dance, flapping their outstretched wings, bobbing their necks up and down, and jumping about excitedly.

Grey crowned cranes in a courting dance.

Breeding dress

Male birds are often more colourful and striking than the females. This is especially true during the breeding season, when some normally drab males develop very bright colours to attract females. The male red-headed weaver and many bishop birds acquire their bright colours only when breeding.

Some males grow flowing tail feathers or a showy collar or breast feathers, all to impress the females.

Long-tailed widowbird

Males grow a spectacular tail that is especially attractive in flight.

Male red-headed weaver — non-breeding / breeding

Male yellow bishop — non-breeding / breeding

The usually drab male ruff grows an ornamental collar in the breeding season.

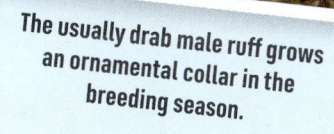

Bright and bobbing

During the breeding season, male tree agamas become a much brighter blue, and display by bobbing their heads up and down, appearing to do push-ups. In this way they attract the attention of females, and also warn competing males to keep their distance.

Scent-marking

Many small antelopes mark out their home territory by rubbing scent, produced by a special gland below the eye, on leaves and branches. They also scent-mark the area with urine and dung, and may scrape the bark of trees with their horns as a marker too. This warns other members of the species to keep away. Territories are where the animals feed, breed and raise their young.

A klipspringer marks its territory using the scent gland below its eye.

Ostrich antics

At the start of the breeding season, ostriches put on a striking show. They call to one another, chase each other wildly, and dance by flapping their outstretched wings and bobbing their heads up and down. Males develop deep pink colouring on their beak and shins and approach the females with a showy walk and then fall to their knees while waving their wings and twisting their neck.

Female ostrich

Male ostrich

DID YOU KNOW? Male and female ostriches have different-coloured plumage. The female's drab brown feathers camouflage her during the day while she protects the eggs. The male takes over nest duty at night, when his mostly black feathers blend with the dark night.

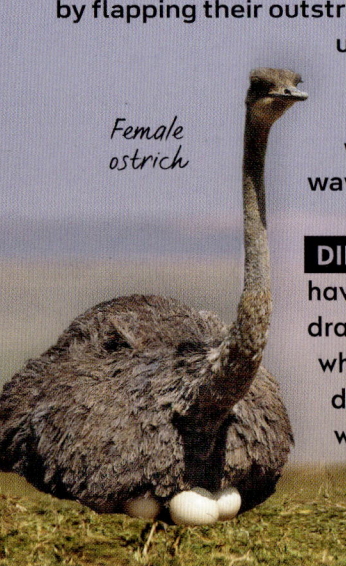

The home makers

Male weaver birds build beautifully woven nests at breeding time and invite passing females to inspect them. Females are very fussy and often reject the work of the males, who then destroy the rejected nest and patiently weave a new one, sometimes again and again, until a female accepts the nest. She will then line the interior with feathers for warmth, and mating follows.

Weaver nests are masterfully built by the male bird, using just his beak.

Sparring zebra stallions

Herds and harems

Zebras live in groups called harems, made up of a single stallion, his females and their young. As young males mature, they are evicted from the herd by the dominant stallion who doesn't want any competition for the females. The young males then form bachelor herds until they reach about five years, when they leave to look for females to 'steal' from established herds and to create harems of their own.

If you see a zebra on its own, it's probably a young male looking for either a bachelor herd to join or a harem from which he can steal a female.

A zebra harem

Serenading songbirds

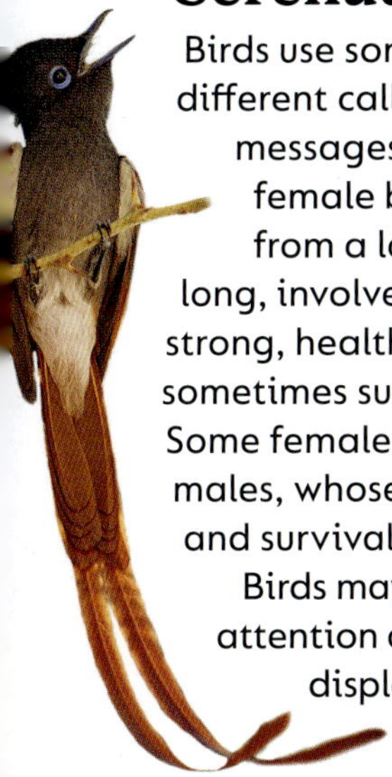

Birds use song during courtship, and different calls communicate different messages. A low-pitched song tells female birds that the sound is coming from a larger and stronger male. A long, involved song is the sign of a strong, healthy and intelligent bird, and sometimes suggests the bird's age too. Some females prefer to mate with older males, whose age is proof of their health and survival skills.

Birds may use other means to draw attention during breeding. In courtship display flights, male African snipes make a whirring sound using stiffened tail feathers, and clapper larks 'clap' their wings together.

Rufous-naped lark

African paradise flycatcher

Bokmakierie

A pair of black-backed jackals

Mates for life

Once they have found their mate, male and female **jackals** and **foxes** remain together and will only seek out a new mate if one of them dies. The pair marks out a territory and will live there permanently and defend it against intruders. The male helps to feed his mate when she has young pups, and as the pups mature, they also help in raising new litters. The offspring leave the family unit once they are old enough to find a mate. **Damara dik-diks** also pair for life and jointly defend their territory. The young are chased out of the family territory when they reach about six months.

Dik-dik pair

Snorts and roars

Impalas live in large herds, headed by a dominant male who breeds with the adult females. At the start of the breeding season, or rut, young males challenge the dominant male, as well as one another, to win the right to mate. They chase and spar with each other, and snort and roar loudly. During the three-week rut, the dominant male hardly eats as he is kept busy marking his territory, fighting off intruders, and mating. He soon weakens and can then be more easily defeated. During this time, a succession of males will take over as head of the herd as each one faces defeat from a stronger opponent.

Young impala rams clash horns in a fight for dominance.

TEST YOUR KNOWLEDGE

Target
How many words can you find? Every word must include the letter in the centre. There is one nine-letter word.

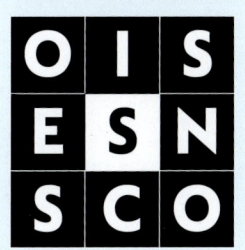

O	I	S
E	**S**	N
S	C	O

Whose horns?
Horns play a big role in conflict and in marking territories. Can you match the horns with these animals?
Bushbuck; Gemsbok; Impala; Klipspringer; Springbok

A B C D E

37

BEATING the heat

Large parts of Africa are very dry and very hot. These include deserts, semi-desert areas and some savanna areas too. Little to no rain falls in these places, and water is generally scarce. Even so, many animals and plants manage to live and grow in these environments.

The Cape ground squirrel uses its bushy tail as a sunshade when the sun beats down.

Evolution — survival of the fittest

Desert plants and animals have evolved over millions of years to survive the harsh conditions. This comes about through the concept of the 'fittest' species being the ones that survive and reproduce. Not all individuals in a species are exactly the same: in any group of plants or animals some will be stronger, some taller, some quicker, and so on. These differences can help or hinder the individuals, depending on the challenges they face in their habitat. Those with the best survival skills for their particular environment have a better chance of surviving and breeding. They then pass along their helpful qualities to their young, while less successful species die out. In this way, animals change, or evolve, over hundreds of years to best fit their environment. This is known as evolution.

A special cooling system

In the heat of the day, the gemsbok's body temperature can rise to an astonishing 45°C, which would kill or severely sicken other antelope species. To prevent the animal's brain reaching this dangerously high temperature, blood is circulated through a network of shallow blood vessels in the area of the nose. As the animal pants, the quick flow of air in and out of the nostrils helps to cool the blood before it flows to the brain.

A network of blood vessels in the gemsbok's nose ensures that blood is cooled before it flows to the brain.

Gemsbok are well equipped to combat the heat and are able to survive in harsh desert conditions.

A cheetah pants to help it cool down.

Marabou stork

Keeping cool

Animals cool themselves in various ways, including panting, sweating and wallowing in mud. Panting moves air rapidly over the moist tongue, mouth and throat. This causes evaporation, which lowers the temperature of the blood flowing through these areas. The cooled blood then flows to the rest of the body. Sweating is another way of offloading heat through evaporation. But for animals in deserts where water is scarce, losing moisture through evaporation is not ideal. The gemsbok saves precious moisture by not sweating (and employs a special cooling system described opposite). Some birds, like the **marabou stork** and **white stork**, beat the heat by defecating on their legs. As the runny, white liquid evaporates, heat is lost, and the birds cool down.

DID YOU KNOW? Hyenas sometimes stand in water deep enough to cool their bellies after they have had a big meal. This protects the body from excess heat caused by the digestive process in the stomach.

Spotted hyena

Water sources

Because there is little or no available water in hot and dry environments, antelopes here get moisture from the grass, leaves and fruit they eat. Most will feed in the early morning and late afternoon, some even at night, when the water content of the grass and other vegetation is at its highest.

DID YOU KNOW? Tsamma melons are relatives of the watermelons that grow in the Kalahari and Namib deserts. These melons are made up of 90% water and so make an ideal meal. They are an important source of water for gemsbok, ground squirrels, some mice, and weavers too.

Efficient ears

Elephants keep cool in a number of ways. Swimming, mud bathing and spraying themselves with water are some of them, but another important method of temperature control involves their ears. An elephant's ears are huge with a fine network of veins at the back, covered by a thin skin layer. Cool air passing over this surface helps to cool the blood in these vessels. The cooled blood is pumped through the elephant's body, bringing down the temperature of the whole animal. Elephants often hold their ears at right angles to allow the air to flow more easily over the back surfaces. Flapping the ears makes this process even more effective.

Some beetles dig trenches to catch droplets of water from passing fog.

Fog-basking beetles

The Namib desert lies along the Atlantic coast of Namibia and Angola. It is the oldest desert and one of the driest places on Earth, as rain is scarce and unpredictable. Nearly all the water needed by animals and plants comes from the fog that rolls in off the ocean. In the early morning, **fog-basking beetles** (a type of 'tok-tokkie' beetle) scuttle to the tops of the dunes and angle their bodies towards the incoming fog, heads lowered and backs lifted into the air. The minute particles of water in the fog cling to the beetles' bodies, forming large water drops that run along their backs and into their mouths.

Namibian fog-basking beetle tilting its body towards the incoming fog

Dancing lizards

Shovel-snouted lizards are the Namib desert's 'dancing reptiles'. When the sand becomes too hot to stand on, they lift opposing feet every few seconds while using their tail for balance. If the heat is unbearable and this special dance is not enough, they use their spade-shaped nose and webbed front feet to dig down below the surface, to where it is cooler. They also dig to bury themselves when escaping from predators and can stay hidden for many hours.

Shovel-snouted lizard

Namaqua chameleon

Dark phase

Living in black and white

The ground-dwelling **Namaqua chameleon** is active during the hot hours of the day. It is able to change the colour of its skin to manage its temperature and cope with the heat. It turns almost black when it needs to warm up, the dark colour helping to absorb the sun's heat very quickly. When it is too hot, its skin becomes pale grey or white, which reflects the sun's warmth and helps the reptile to cool down.

Pale phase

Sand snakes

The desert-dwelling sidewinder snake is an ambush hunter and buries itself just beneath the surface of the sand with its eyes and very little else of its body visible. Passing lizards and geckos are snapped up and eaten. The snake obtains moisture from its prey, and from water that collects on its body from the fog that moves in from the ocean.

A flightless dung beetle hurries to its sandy burrow.

Swimming in the dune sea

At a depth of about 300mm, the sand of the Namib Desert starts to become cooler. An array of small animals, known as 'evaders', copes with extreme heat by hiding beneath the sand during the hot daylight hours. These are most commonly insects, spiders and scorpions, but there are also some mammals that live in the 'sand sea' of the Namib. The **Namib golden mole** and the **hairy-footed dune gerbil** come out only at night, to forage. Both species have feet that are modified for scraping, so that they can 'swim' through the sand below the surface.

Word puzzle

Fit the words into the grid

Gemsbok   Hyena   Marabou
Fog   Adder   Ear
Desert   Tsamma Water

S A N D G R O U S E

Water delivery

Sandgrouse fly as much as 60km in the early morning to reach waterholes and pans where they drink. When chicks are very young and unable to fly, the male birds soak their breast and belly feathers at the water before flying back. The 'waterlogged' fathers then return to the chicks and fluff out their feathers so the young birds can drink the trapped water.

Sandgrouse prefer arid areas, but do need access to water and will fly great distances to reach it.

Family LIFE

The main challenge of life in the wild is survival — not only survival of individuals, but survival of species. Animals raise and defend their young in different ways.

Elephant herd

In **elephant** communities, the whole herd takes responsibility for protecting, teaching and raising the young. When a pregnant female is ready to give birth, the family gathers around her to guard her and the calf from danger. Once the baby elephant is born, other females help it get to its feet and find its mother's milk. Later, the youngster will learn what to eat by watching its mother and its aunts. Younger females also help to look after the babies and so gain the skills and experience they will need to become mothers themselves.

Lioness and cub

Baby elephant suckling

Big cat families

Lions live in family groups called prides, which comprise from two to 12 related adult females and their cubs; adult males join a pride temporarily for breeding purposes. All male cubs leave the pride at two to four years of age. The males often band together in all-male groups until they are strong enough to set out alone and take over a territory.

Unlike lions, **leopards** and **cheetahs** live alone. While their cubs are small, mothers will feed and care for them, and teach them to hunt before they set out to live their own lives. Leopards leave their mother at about two years old. Cheetahs remain with their mother until they are about 18 months, when they are almost as large as she is. Siblings usually stay together for several months until the females are old enough to breed.

Leopard mothers move their cubs from den to den to keep them safe from predators.

Cheetah and cub

Mother and child

Can you match the babies to their species?

YOUNG		ADULT	
A Kitten	F Gosling	1 Goose	6 Porcupine
B Infant	G Foal	2 Beetle	7 Elephant
C Grub	H Hatchling	3 Crocodile	8 Warthog
D Calf	I Wriggler	4 Baboon	9 Mosquito
E Piglet	J Porcupette	5 Serval	10 Zebra

What am I called?

Some pack members babysit the pups while the others go hunting.

Nature's nurseries

African wild dogs live in packs led by an alpha male and alpha female. They are the only ones that breed, while the rest of the pack helps to raise the pups. When the pack is out hunting, the pups remain at the den and some pack members stay behind to babysit them. The hunting adults will eat as much as they can, and on returning to the den regurgitate a meal for the pups and their babysitters.

Bat-eared fox cubs also have a babysitter. While the mother is out feeding, the father guards the young. This ensures that the mother is well nourished so that she can nurse the pups until they are big enough to forage alone.

Bat-eared foxes

DID YOU KNOW? African wild dogs and foxes are not the only animals with a 'crèche'. Some herbivores leave their young in 'nursery herds' that are cared for by other adults. Young giraffe calves are left with a single adult carer while the other females forage and drink.

Lessons for life

Lion cubs playing

Play fighting teaches young animals special skills they need to survive in later life. In this way, young predators learn their first lessons about hunting. The twitch of a tail sees them jumping to 'attack' it, and they stalk and pounce on their siblings during mock attacks. In some species, such as **foxes**, play fighting involves competing for food. From just one week old, young foxes push and shove to get to their mother's milk, and soon they compete for the scraps of solid food that she offers them.

Cape fox pups playing

The white circle on the rump of a waterbuck provides a 'target' for the young to follow, ensuring that families stay together.

Follow the leader

Warthog families make an orderly retreat when they are startled. The adult male leads the way with his long, thin tail up in the air. The tuft of hair at the end is a beacon for the rest of the family. The female follows, and the young warthogs fall in line behind them.

Baboons bond by grooming each other.

Family grooming

Monkeys, **baboons** and **bushbabies** take much longer to become independent than do the young of other mammals. Their mothers carry them around and groom them to keep them clean. Grooming not only helps to keep ticks and fleas away, it also strengthens the bond between mother and infant. Adult baboons secure the bonds between troop members by grooming one another too, combing the fur of others with their fingers to remove dust and dirt, ticks and other parasites.

Mom's taxi

Several animals carry their newborn young from place to place. As soon as **scorpion** nymphs are born, they clamber onto their mother, and stay on her back for up to three weeks. It's the only way she can feed and protect up to a hundred babies while their outer shells (exoskeletons) are still soft.

If the water is too deep for a **hippo** calf to stand in, the mother will support the youngster on her back.

Female baboons carry their babies with them, first under their belly and later on their back.

Dabchick (or little grebe) babies ride on their parents' backs, nestling in the dry warm feathers. They hold their breath and cling on when the adult birds dive to chase after prey under water.

A hippo cow bears only one calf every two or three years, and is caring and protective of it as it grows up.

Insect parents

Some animals spend years raising just one youngster, making sure it grows up well. Others, especially insects, have many offspring, and put little effort into parenting — the odds are that at least some will survive. **Termites** hold the reproduction record. The enormously fat queen lays up to 10,000 eggs every day for over 20 years.

Termite queen

Who am I?

I have the most fearsome jaws in the whole animal kingdom, but they can also be used gently. I protect my buried eggs for months. When the babies begin to hatch they make chirping noises, which I hear. I dig up the nest, take the newborn hatchlings in my mouth, and carry them safely to water.

Cold-blooded mothers

Many snakes abandon their eggs after they have been laid, leaving the hatchlings to fend for themselves. But **southern African python** mothers are more caring. They lay their eggs in an underground nest and keep the eggs warm until they hatch. For the first few weeks, newborn pythons venture out by day to bask in the sun but return at night to keep warm between their mother's coils.

A python mother warms her young with her body.

Dutiful dads

A female **African jacana** can produce up to 30 clutches of eggs each year. As soon as she has laid her eggs, she abandons them to look for another mate, leaving the nest under the care of the father. The male incubates the eggs and, once they have hatched, keeps the chicks warm and dry under his wings as they grow up. If danger threatens, he will quickly scoop them up beneath his wings and carry them to a safer place.

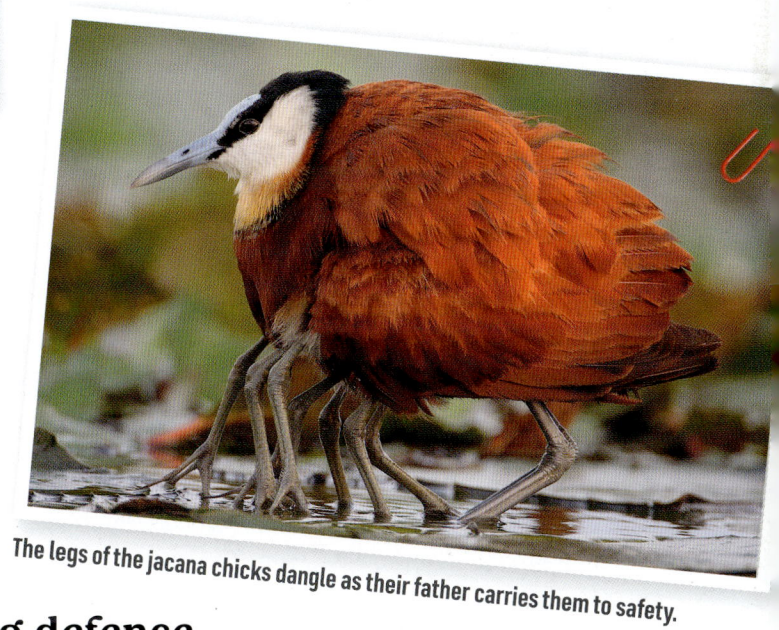

The legs of the jacana chicks dangle as their father carries them to safety.

Daring defence

Some bird parents defend their young fiercely. The nest of a **crowned lapwing** is no more than a shallow scrape in the ground, lined with sticks, grass and leaves. Eggs and newly hatched chicks are therefore vulnerable to snakes, secretarybirds, marabou storks and other predators. If danger approaches, a parent bird will pretend to be injured, sometimes dragging what appears to be a broken wing, so that the predator will chase it instead of getting to the nest. If the predator does approach the chicks, the parent birds become noisy and aggressive, often dive-bombing the intruder to chase it away.

A crowned lapwing spreads its wings in a threat display as a snake edges towards its nest.

NESTS & DENS

Nests and dens provide safety and warmth, and are places in which to lay eggs and to protect and raise young. They can range from simple hollows in the ground to deep underground burrows, and from nests in trees to towering mud structures above the ground.

Colossal colonies

Sociable weavers build the biggest nests of any birds. The nest is made up of separate chambers, one for each 'family unit'. Unlike other weaver nests that are newly built each breeding season, these are permanent nests and are used for both roosting and breeding. The nest offers a cool escape from the heat of the day and a warm retreat on chilly nights.

Sociable weavers are found only in southern Africa.

Sociable weaver nest

DID YOU KNOW?
Other small birds, such as this rosy-faced lovebird, use sociable weaver nests too.

Holing in the hornbill

The **southern yellow-billed hornbill** has one of the most curious nesting habits. After mating, a male and female bird seek out a hole in a tree trunk, which they line with leaves and bark. The female enters and seals herself inside, leaving just a small gap though which the male bird will feed her, while she lays her eggs and protects the chicks. When the chicks are a few weeks old, the mother leaves the nest, seals it up again, and both parents take turns to feed the chicks.

The male bird feeds the female through a small gap.

CRAFTY CUCKOOS

Some species of cuckoo are brood parasites. They don't build their own nests, instead laying their eggs in other birds' nests — to be fed and raised by another set of parents.

This large common cuckoo chick is in a reed warbler's nest and is being fed by its adoptive mother.

46

The great crested grebe builds a floating nest.

Little ringed plover nest and eggs.

On land and on water

Some birds, such as **grebes** and **coots**, build a floating platform nest to hold their eggs and prevent them from sinking. **Flamingos** use their beak to shape mud into a cone-shaped nest. A few bird species get away with not building a nest at all. **Plovers** and **thick-knees** lay eggs in a shallow scrape in the sand. Their eggs are cleverly patterned to blend with the surrounding ground.

Nesting flamingos

Insect homes

Most **ants**, **termites**, **wasps** and **bees** build communal nests, some with special 'rooms' for the queen and her eggs. Among the most spectacular are termite mounds that rise high above the ground. They are built from mud, dung and saliva, and are used over many years by different generations. The mound is built above an underground nest chamber, and inside it is a maze of tunnels.

Abandoned termite mounds become resting and look-out spots for other animals, like this leopard.

Burrow borrowers

The unusual **aardvark** is found only in Africa. It uses its very strong legs and sharp claws to dig a burrow in which to shelter and raise its young. When these burrows are abandoned they often become homes for other animals, including Cape porcupines, warthogs, aardwolves and pangolins.

A warthog rests in an old aardvark home.

An aardvark in its burrow

At the water

Spend a quiet hour or two next to a river, dam or waterhole to watch a procession of wildlife. Most animals gather here in the early morning and late afternoon, when it is cooler.

Keeping cool

Rivers, dams and pools are gathering points where animals drink and feed; but some, such as **hippos**, take to the water for hours just to keep cool. **Elephants** love water too, not just to drink but to bathe in, to play in, and to spray over their body.

For **buffaloes**, the more mud the better — they wallow for hours. These bulky beasts are very sensitive to heat, and the mud covering their body protects them from sunburn and from insect bites.

Buffaloes use mud as sunscreen.

Beware the hippo

While lolling in the water, hippos are usually lazy and peaceful, although there are occasional clashes between males who want to show their strength. They stretch their mouth wide open, showing their large tusks to intimidate their rivals. These teeth are used only for slashing and biting in combat, not for feeding at all. Hippos are known to attack people too — campers and rural dwellers that come between a hippo and its territory risk being attacked and trampled. Hippos are probably responsible for more than 500 human deaths every year.

On cool days hippos move to the banks to bask.

DID YOU KNOW? A hippo mother will fiercely defend her baby against any predator that comes too close. With her powerful jaws she could bite a crocodile in half.

Dangerous drinking holes

Prey animals, such as antelopes and zebras, are wary of predators and always approach water cautiously. Not all members in a group drink at the same time — some keep a lookout for danger to allow others to drink first. Larger mammals like buffaloes and elephants can be very aggressive at water, especially if they have young. They will chase away other species, even predators, allowing their herd to drink and wallow safely. All animals need to be on the alert for crocodiles that might be lurking in the shallows. Even lions fall prey to these fearsome reptiles.

The waders

Storks and herons are large, long-legged birds that wade slowly and patiently through shallow water in search of fishes, crabs and frogs. The **black heron** uses a clever method to catch fish. The bird tucks its head down, spreads its wings around its body, and creates a canopy of shade. Small fishes looking for places to hide are attracted to the shade only to be quickly snapped up. The mandibles (top and bottom parts of the bill) of the **African openbill** meet only at the tip, leaving a wide gap between them. The bird grips its snail prey between the mandibles, holds the snail against the ground, and then uses its razor-sharp bottom mandible to pry the flesh from the shell.

Black heron fishing

African openbill

The fishers

Rivers and dams are an important source of food for many birds. A special resident of large stretches of water is the **African fish eagle**, a stately bird of prey often seen perched on top of a tall tree. It has strong, sharp talons that prevent even the most slippery fish from wriggling free. Listen out for its distinctive clear call, known to some as 'the voice of Africa'. **Kingfishers** are common residents at water too. They hunt from perches, diving into the water to snatch fish.

African fish eagle

Pied kingfisher

Who am I?

Look closely at the markings, faces and bills of these aquatic birds. Can you match the numbered birds to the names?

A Great crested grebe
B Red-billed teal
C White-faced whistling duck
C Egyptian goose
E Red-knobbed coot
F Knob-billed duck

Tunnel dwellers

Ever seen clusters of round holes in riverbanks? These are the nest-tunnels of the colourful **bee-eaters**. Most bee-eater species nest in colonies. Despite their name, they don't eat only bees. Other insects, especially locusts and dragonflies that live and breed around water, are an important part of their diet. Bee-eaters grab their prey in flight, then beat it or rub it against a branch to kill it. This behaviour also helps to remove the stings from bees and wasps.

European bee-eaters

Red-throated bee-eaters breed and feed along the riverbank.

Large lizards

The **water monitor** is a huge, dragon-like reptile with powerful legs, claws and tail. It uses its long tail as a whip against attackers. This lizard is common along rivers and around dams, where it forages for crabs, frogs, eggs, small mammals and waterbirds. Its mottled colouring provides effective camouflage, enabling it to remain hidden from predators and to stalk prey unnnoticed.

Nile water monitor

TINY TERRAPINS

Terrapins are easy to miss at a waterhole. These small freshwater reptiles often bask motionless in the sun, looking like smooth stones. They can sometimes be seen picking ticks and flies off wallowing buffaloes and hippos. Terrapins defend themselves with sharp claws and powerful jaws which are strong enough to bite off a human finger.

Some terrapins have a hinged shell that can open and close. They withdraw their head and limbs, then shut the shell for protection.

Amphibian life

Most frogs and toads begin their lives in water as tadpoles and move onto land as their lungs and legs grow. The giant **African bullfrog** grows to a length of 200mm — almost as big as a dinner plate. It is an aggressive carnivore with sharp teeth, and eats rodents, birds and reptiles.

The **foam nest frog** is another interesting amphibian. The female deposits a liquid that contains hundreds of eggs on a branch overhanging water. With her hind legs, she churns this liquid into a foam. When the tadpoles hatch, they drop into the water below.

The African bullfrog has sharp teeth, and will give a painful bite if you try to pick it up.

The foam nest frog lays its eggs on branches that overhang water.

Platanna

DID YOU KNOW? Frogs, such as the platanna, can breathe on land and under water. In water, their thin skin allows oxygen to pass directly into the body.

MENACING MOZZIES

Mosquitoes also gather around water, especially stagnant water, where they lay their eggs. They don't need much of it — a small puddle is enough. Mosquitoes feed on flower nectar and plant sap, but female mosquitoes feed on blood as well. One group, known as *Anopheles* mosquitoes, causes the spread of malaria among humans. A bite from an *Anopheles* female transfers infected blood from one person to another.

Walking on water

At the edges of the water, **fishing spiders** lurk with their front legs resting on the surface to sense vibrations. When they detect movement, they dash across the water to make their kill. These spiders are covered in water-repellent hairs, so they can walk on the water surface with their legs spread wide apart, and even hunt underwater, where they breathe in the air trapped between their body hairs. They mostly eat insects and tadpoles, but some bigger species catch small frogs and fishes too.

Six-spotted fishing spider

51

NIGHT life

When night falls in the bush, a new world comes to life. Animals, birds, frogs, scorpions and insects that sleep or hide by day come out after sunset to hunt and feed. Some are usually heard rather than seen, but the bush can be a busy place at night.

Why choose the night?
Less competition Animals avoid competition for food by being active at different times.
Safety Moving under cover of darkness means that animals are less visible and can avoid being discovered, whether they are predators in search of prey, or a prey animal avoiding a predator.
It's cooler at night Animals save energy by working in the cooler night-time hours

Hyenas hunt at night and rest by day.

- Animals that are active at night are known as **nocturnal**.
- **Diurnal** animals are most active by day. They include baboons, elephants, rhinos, warthogs, antelopes and most birds.
- Animals that are active at dawn and dusk are called **crepuscular** animals.

PREDATORS ON THE PROWL

Many mammal predators have adapted to hunt at night. Lions have eyes that are adapted to the dark, giving them an advantage over their prey. Hyenas also have excellent night vision and mostly hunt at night, using daytime hours to rest or sleep. Other nocturnal predators include genets, civets and smaller cat species.

Genet

Bushbabies

Bushbabies, also called galagos, or *nagapies* in Afrikaans, are nocturnal tree-dwellers. They have big round eyes that allow more light in to help them see better at night, and their large, cupped ears are adapted to track and trace insect prey. They also eat tree gum and fruit. Other adaptations include strong back legs for jumping between branches, and large hands and feet, padded at the finger and toe tips to provide good grip. Bushbabies wee on their hands and feet to scent mark well-used routes within their territories, making it quick to get around.

DID YOU KNOW? Bushbabies communicate with many different calls. One is a wailing sound that gives them their name; it sounds just like a human baby crying.

Thick-tailed bushbaby

Light is reflected from the large round eyes of the bushbaby.

Insect-eating bat

Fruit-eating bat

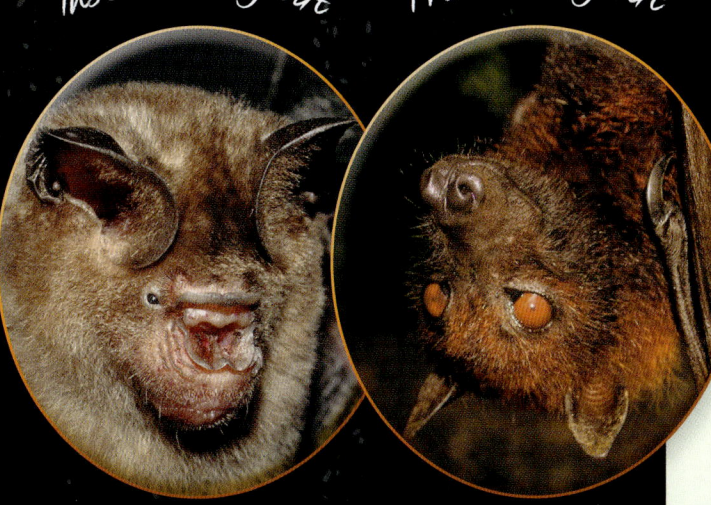

Blind as a bat?

Insect-eating bats rely on their ears instead of their eyes to find their way in the dark. But not all bats have poor eyesight: fruit-eating bats see very well. They are bigger than insect-eaters and have long-muzzled faces that make them look a bit like dogs. Bats navigate using echo-location: they make high-pitched squeaks that bounce back off hard surfaces. By listening to the echoes, the bats can fly in total darkness without hitting any obstacles.

DID YOU KNOW? Bats hang upside down because their legs are too weak to support them. Their claws automatically close on the surface to which they cling — there is no effort involved.

Digging for dinner

Aardvarks are strictly nocturnal and emerge from their burrows after dark. They have excellent senses of smell and hearing, which they use to avoid predators and to detect their termite and ant prey. They break open nests with their powerful front legs and claws, and then lick up the insects with their long, sticky tongue. They have thick hair around their nostrils to help keep out sand as they dig. The aardvark's skin is especially thick, to protect it from bites and stings.

Aardvark

Aardvark cucumbers

DID YOU KNOW? Aardvarks also use their strong legs and claws to dig up aardvark cucumbers. These provide all the moisture the animals need so they can survive without water if necessary.

CALLS OF THE NIGHT

- Hoot of the owl
- Rasp of a leopard
- Laugh of the hyena
- Cry of the jackal
- Croaks and squeaks of the frogs
- Roar of the lion
- Chirrups of crickets

The rasp of a leopard sounds like dry wood being sawed.

Night-time grazers

Most antelopes feed in the early morning and late afternoon, but a few species are almost fully nocturnal feeders. Reedbuck are shy and solitary, and rest in dense bushy cover most of the day, coming out at sunset to feed. Gemsbok and eland, which do not depend on surface water for drinking, graze at night when the moisture content in the leaves and grass they eat is higher.

Gemsbok

Shining scorpions

Scorpions have exoskeletons (skeletons outside their bodies — like the 'shell' of a crab) that glow blue-green under an ultra-violet flashlight.

Birds of the night

Night birds have large eyes that enable them to see in low-light conditions. They rely on their excellent eyesight and sensitive hearing to find food. Bright colours are of no use in the dark, so nocturnal birds are usually drab in colour, which also helps them remain camouflaged by day.

European nightjar

Nightjars have soft-edged wings, which help them to fly silently while hunting. They feed in flight, searching with their huge eyes for flying insects.

Owls have good night vision — but it's their hearing that makes them deadly nocturnal hunters. If an owl hears a noise and is not facing its prey directly, any sound the prey makes will take longer to reach one of the owl's ears than the other, because the sound has a very slightly longer distance to travel. The owl slowly turns its head until the sound reaches both ears at exactly the same time, and then it knows its prey is directly in front of it.

Cape eagle owl

Black-crowned night heron

Night herons are cunning ambush hunters. They often stir the water with their bill, and throw bits of grass or small sticks onto the water, to make ripples. Fish coming to explore the movement swim straight into a trap.

The NIGHT sky

The Milky Way is a hazy band of stars seen across the night sky. It is the galaxy in which our sun and all the planets around it are found. The Milky Way is more easily seen outside the cities, where nights are darker.

The bush is the best place for stargazing because, away from the distracting glare of town and city lights, the skies are much darker and the stars much brighter.

Stars and constellations

Stars are clustered in groups in the sky. These groups are called **constellations** and have their own names. Two of the best-known constellations are the Southern Cross and Orion, the Hunter with his distinctive three-star belt.

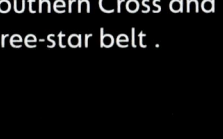

Orion's belt

Orion, the Hunter

Scorpio

Southern Cross

Pointers

This is south

Find south using the stars

The **Southern Cross** is a constellation with four major stars that roughly form a cross. It is visible from southern Africa all year. Two bright 'pointer stars' a little to one side help to confirm you have found the Southern Cross. To find south, imagine two lines being drawn, one starting from the head down through the foot of the cross, and one from the middle of a line that joins the pointers. South is where the two lines meet.

Star or planet?

Heavenly bodies that twinkle are stars. They make their own light because they are suns, like our sun. Heavenly bodies that don't twinkle are planets. Planets shine with light reflected from our sun, so they appear in the sky as a steady light.

55

Scat FACTS

Animal droppings are an important part of wild areas, and every scat has a tale to tell. Droppings can give you information about the sex, movement and diet of an animal.

Rhinos drop their dung at communal middens.

A hippo expels and scatters its dung.

Making your mark

Many mammals use their urine and dung to communicate with other animals. Dung, and where it is placed, can serve to mark a territory, warn off intruders, or indicate that a female in the group is ready to mate. Some species, like civets, have communal latrines, which they use repeatedly. Others, like jackals and foxes, make their droppings easily visible by depositing them on small shrubs, grass clumps and rocks. When marking their territories, male hippos flick their tails like very fast windscreen wipers to scatter their dung.

Dung beetles

If you find a pile of droppings strewn about, it may be the work of dung beetles. These busy little creatures depend on dung for food and for breeding. Some beetles shape the dung into a ball and roll it away to bury at some distance. The female then lays an egg inside the ball. To move these balls, which can be ten times the weight of a beetle, the insect scuttles backward in a handstand pose, with its forelegs on the ground and its hindlegs on the ball.

Elephant droppings are first prize for dung beetles.

Dung beetle

DID YOU KNOW? Many animals use the position of the sun and moon to navigate, but South African scientists have discovered that dung beetles use the stars to find their way at night.

Whose poo?

The shape, size, colour, content and location of droppings are all clues as to which animal left them, but it is not always easy to identify the exact species. Sometimes a general identification will have to do — for example, identifying the scat of a big cat, rather than a lion or leopard specifically.

Large, barrel-shaped droppings are deposited by elephants and rhinos. When fresh, they are dark and damp, with a fibrous texture from the grass and leaves the animals eat. Rhino droppings are smaller and found in middens (communal dung heaps).

Elephant dung

HOW FRESH? If you break open elephant dung and discover it is dry all the way through, you'll know it's at least six hours old.

Kidney-shaped droppings are from zebras, warthogs and bushpigs. They are green or brown when fresh, and darken with age.

Bushpig droppings

Sausage-shaped, pointed droppings are left by civets, genets, mongooses, jackals, foxes and African wild dogs. They are usually found in large quantities in latrines, and contain insect remains, feathers, rodent hair and small bones.

Genet poop

Sausage-shaped, segmented droppings are from hyenas and aardwolf as well as cats. The segments are held together by hair. Hyenas use latrines, where their scat quickly dries white because of the bone content. Cats randomly deposit their faeces, which are initially dark to black from the blood of their prey.

Spotted hyena scat

> Herbivores 'plant' new trees, shrubs and grasses by eating seeds that can't be broken down in their stomach, and are instead deposited in their droppings.

The long drop
Giraffes leave large, round pellets, usually in piles of about ten.

Bird and reptile droppings often have a white coating or blob next to the main dropping. The white is uric acid, which is expelled through the same opening as the more solid dropping.

Guineafowl droppings

Puff adder poop

Pellets are left by antelopes, giraffes and many smaller mammals. They vary in size and shape, from large and roughly round (large antelopes and giraffes) to small and round (small antelopes, rabbits and hares) or tiny and cylindrical (bats, rats and mice).

Klipspringer pellets

Flat, circular 'pats' are from buffaloes. The green-brown dung (drying to black) is originally almost liquid, and forms a rippled pancake shape as it hits the ground and spreads.

Buffalo pat

57

Tracks & signs

Wherever animals go, they leave signs of their presence. Footprints and other evidence reveal that animals were there, and could still be nearby.

Tracks can be detected by carefully examining the ground.

Carnivore tracks show a pad and usually four toes.

- 🐾 **African Wild Dogs** have claw marks at the ends of the toes, typical of dog-like feet.
- 🐾 **The caracal**, a true cat, has fully retractible claws that don't show up in their tracks.
- 🐾 **The Cape clawless otter** has five toes. Its front feet have no nails or claws.

African wild dog *Caracal* *Cape clawless otter* (Front / Hind)

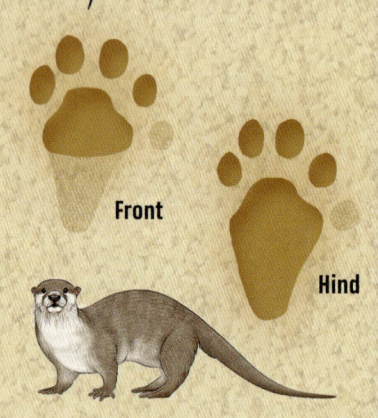

Cloven-hoofed animals have a split or 'cleft' hoof. They include **antelopes, giraffes, pigs** and **buffaloes**. It takes a lot of practice to know exactly which antelope made a track, but size is a good clue. Giraffe and buffaloes leave the biggest tracks.

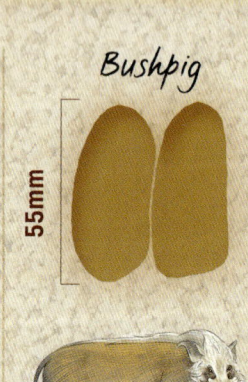

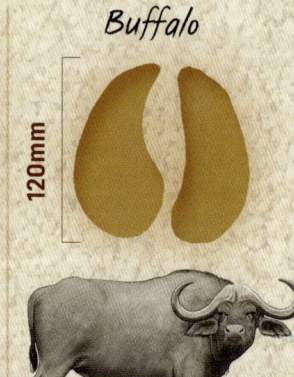

Steenbok 39mm *Giraffe* 200mm *Bushpig* 55mm *Buffalo* 120mm

Early morning news

? Sweep a smooth patch of ground outside your bungalow last thing before you go to bed at night. If you wake up early the next morning you might find tracks that tell you who your visitors were during the night.
Can you tell which animals made these tracks?

The single big, curved toe at the front of the **zebra's** hoof looks like that of a horse and is easy to recognise.

Birds have four toes, usually three pointing forward and one backwards. Often only the front three toes leave marks.

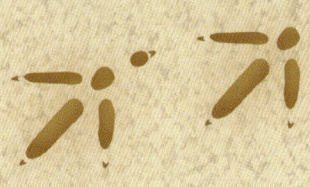

Helmeted guineafowl

Primates all have five toes on each foot, but the toes usually show up more clearly in hind-foot tracks.

Vervet monkey — Front / Hind

EVER SEEN ONE OF THESE?
This small pit in the sand is the trap of an **antlion larva**. If an ant or other small insect wanders near to the edge of the pit, it will slide down in a little sand avalanche to the hole at the bottom, where the larva is waiting to pounce.

Antlion larva

HIPPO versus RHINO
The **hippo's** foot has four clear toes. Both **rhino** species have three toes on each foot, which are not as clearly divided as the hippo's.

Desert-dwelling beetles leave distinctive tracks in loose sand.

Most snakes move in a sideways fashion, leaving wavy tracks. Heavier snakes, such as pythons and adders, move in a straight line.

59

An elephant's back foot is five times bigger than this.

Front foot at 100%

Elephant tracks are the largest of all African animal tracks. The front feet are larger and rounded while the hind feet leave oval-shaped prints. The tracks often show a pattern of cracks and ridges, reflecting the thick soles of the feet.

Rubbing posts

When an elephant has an itch it will rub itself against a convenient rock or tree trunk. Repeated use of these 'rubbing posts' wears away the surface and makes them smooth and shiny.

OTHER SIGNS IN THE WILD

Loose quills indicate that a porcupine has been in the area.

Dried out bones and skulls tell of a kill that took place, and what animal suffered at the jaws of a predator.

Rhinos are also fond of using trees as rubbing posts to scratch an itch.

White markings seen on a rock face indicate the presence of a raptor's nest. The birds' repeated droppings build up, leaving white patches.

Keep an eye out for scratch marks on tree trunks. Big cats often sharpen their claws on these surfaces, leaving signs of their presence.

A skin layer that has been shed is a sure sign of a snake in the area.

61

Answers

Page 5
SHARP SIGHT 1. Zebra; 2. Lion; 3. Elephant; 4. Scops owl; 5. Southern African python

Page 7
ANIMAL ANAGRAMS 1. Leopard; 2. Springhare; 3. Bat; 4. Dassie; 5. Giraffe; 6. Badger; 7. Civet; 8. Lion

Page 9
WORD LADDER
1. FLAP – FLOP – FLOW – GLOW
2. CORK – FORK – FORT – FOOT

Page 15
JIZZ A. Sunbird; B. Heron; C. Guineafowl; D. Owl; E. Vulture F. Dove

WORD PUZZLE

				P	A	R	R	O	T
	V			R					
G	U	I	N	E	A	F	O	W	L
	L			E		L			
	T			N		A			B
	U					M			U
C	R	O	W		J	I	Z	Z	
	E		I			N			Z
			N			G			A
			G			O			R
O	W	L	S						D

Page 20
FOOD OR FOE? C and E, but not B, the scorpion. A suricate won't run from a scorpion — it would much rather eat it.

Page 21
CLEVER CAMOUFLAGE 1. Viper; 2. Cheetah; 3. Chameleon; 4. Spider; 5. Dwarf mongoose; 6. Nightjar

Page 23
WHO AM I? 1. Eland; 2. Giraffe; 3. Zebra; 4. Honey badger; 5. Tsessebe; 6. Springbok

Page 26
DUNG MAZE

Page 27
MISSING LETTERS 1. Cud; 2. Tongue; 3. Browse; 4. Tusk; 5. Mutualism

Page 29
WORD SEARCH

A	T	R	S	P	E	E	D	P	R	O	P	A	C	K
C	L	A	W	I	F	E	D	O	P	R	E	Y	T	P
O	S	P	C	H	A	S	E	U	D	A	T	P	A	R
L	T	T	P	R	N	C	A	N	S	P	R	Y	L	H
R	A	O	O	C	G	R	T	C	A	T	A	M	O	U
Y	L	R	F	F	O	T	H	E	C	O	C	L	N	N
P	K	X	P	R	E	D	A	T	O	R	K	I	L	T

Page 30
LITTLE HUNTERS 1. Cape fox; 2. African civet; 3. Small-spotted genet; 4. African wild cat

Page 31
ODD ONE OUT The darter is not a raptor.

Page 37
WHOSE HORNS? A. Impala; B. Bushbuck; C. Klipspringer; D. Springbok; E. Gemsbok

TARGET The nine-letter word is Ossicones.

Page 41
WORD PUZZLE

				W		T	S	A	M	M	A
				A				A			
				T		D		R			
	G		E			E		A			
E	A	R				S		B			H
M			A			E		O			Y
S	A	N	D	G	R	O	U	S	E		
B			D			T					N
F	O	G		E							A
K				R							

Page 43
MOTHER AND CHILD A. Kitten — Serval; B. Infant — Baboon; C. Grub — Beetle; D. Calf — Elephant; E. Piglet — Warthog; F. Gosling — Goose; G. Foal — Zebra; H. Hatchling — Crocodile; I. Wriggler — Mosquito; J. Porcupette — Porcupine

Page 45
WHO AM I? A crocodile

Page 50
WHO AM I? 1. White-faced whistling duck; 2. Red-knobbed coot; 3. Knob-billed duck; 4. Red-billed teal; 5. Great crested grebe; 6. Egyptian goose

Page 58
EARLY MORNING NEWS A lion has visited in the night.

Glossary

Alpha (male/female) The individual in a group with most authority; the leader; often the only member of that sex in the group that is allowed to breed.

Ambush Lying hidden in wait for prey and catching it by surprise when it is close enough.

Bushveld Grassy plains with trees and dense clusters of tall shrubs. Bushveld is a type of savanna whose trees and shrubs grow very close together, and not as tall as the trees of a fully mature savanna.

Camouflage The colours and markings that make it difficult to see an animal in its natural surroundings.

Carrion Dead meat; the remains of an animal's carcass.

Dominant Being the strongest or most senior or most powerful animal in a group, who is able to move, feed and breed without hindrance from other members of the group.

Droppings A general term for animal poo.

Endangered Being at risk of becoming extinct because one's population is getting smaller (often because of hunting and poaching, or over-harvesting), and habitat is being taken over for human use. Such a species needs to be protected.

Estuary The widening channel of a river as it flows into the sea. At high tide, salty water flows back up the estuary.

Evaporation This happens when a liquid turns into a gas or vapour as a result of heat, such as in a dry or hot environment. Evaporation uses up standing water that animals need to drink.

Evolution The gradual change in a species as it becomes better suited to living in a particular environment.

Foraging Searching for wild food in the environment, usually plant material (like seeds and berries) or insects (like ants).

Habitat The physical environment in which a species naturally lives.

Home range The area that an animal or group occupies and moves around in. Unlike a 'territory', animals don't defend home ranges against intruders or competitors.

Harem A group of animals consisting of one (or occasionally two) males, a number of females and their offspring. The dominant male chases off other males who try to join the group or attract the females away.

Incubate To keep newly laid eggs warm to enable them to hatch. Birds sit on their eggs in the nest to do this — it is also called 'brooding'. Other animals, like turtles and crocodiles, incubate their eggs by burying them to keep them warm.

Mimicry Having physical features that closely imitate those of another species (such as a non-poisonous frog or insect looking like a poisonous one) or objects (like tree twigs), for both defence and attack.

Opportunism The ability of a species to live and thrive in many different conditions and environments, making the most of whatever opportunities present themselves for feeding and breeding.

Organism Any living thing, such as a plant, animal or fungus.

Parasite An organism (plant or animal) that lives on (or with) another organism, and harms that host by taking its food or its energy.

Poaching Illegal killing of animals that don't belong to you, for food or to sell.

Pollination/Pollinate The transfer by water, wind or animal movements of pollen from a male plant to a female plant, to fertilise the female plant and enable it to bear seeds and reproduce.

Raptor A hunting bird that catches live food in its powerful talons.

Savanna A grassland with scattered trees, usually tall and widely spaced, or closer together but not close enough to block out the sun from the grass below.

Scat The droppings of wild animals, especially those of large cats.

Scavenger Any animal that searches for and feeds mainly on dead organisms; such as carnivores eating another animal's kill, or insects eating dead plant material.

Solitary An animal that generally lives alone (except to breed) rather than in a pair or a group.

Species The biggest group of organisms that is able to breed and produce offspring. Buffalo weavers are a species, but they don't breed with, for instance, Cape weavers, which are a separate species.

Territory An area claimed by an animal in which to live and operate, and which it will defend from intruders competing for food and shelter.

Picture credits

BDP = Bernard DUPONT, CC BY-SA 2.0, WC
IOA = Images of Africa
JS = Jennifer Schaum
OH = Owen Hendry
PH = Peter Hayman
PRH = Penguin Random House
SM = Sally MacLarty
WC = via Wikimedia Commons
b = bottom, c = centre, l = left, m = middle, r = right, t = top

All tracks throughout the book © PRH
Front cover: background sky © andreusK - stock.adobe.com, **tl** Ron Knight, CC BY-SA 2.0, WC, **tr** Sergio Pozzetti, WC, **ml** © anankkml - stock.adobe.com, **mr** BDP, **background leaf** Ilmicro from Pixabay, **bl** Four Oaks/Shutterstock.com, **br** © Samuel B. - stock.adobe.com
Back cover: t BDP, **ml** © dennisjacobsen - stock.adobe.com, **mr** © Lennart - stock.adobe.com, **bl** © PACO COMO - stock.adobe.com, **bm** © anthony - stock.adobe.com, **br** Mathias Appel, WC
Title: Marie Stone/KOKO - stock.adobe.com
Contents: t © PRH, **b** © stuporter - stock.adobe.com
4: mammals SM/© PRH, **birds** PH/© PRH, **all other illustrations** © SM, **pride of lions** © Nick Dale - stock.adobe.com
5: tr © LMspencer - stock.adobe.com, **mr** © PACO COMO - stock.adobe.com, **1.** OH, **2.** Lisa H on Unsplash.com, **3.** © Anton Ivanov Photo - stock.adobe.com, **4.** © creativenature.nl - stock.adobe.com, **5.** © Nick Dale - stock.adobe.com, **br** © WakebreakMediaMicro - stock.adobe.com
6: tr © EcoView - stock.adobe.com, **ml** © Chaithanya - stock.adobe.com, **mr** © ondrejprosicky - stock.adobe.com, **bl** © Nick Dale - stock.adobe.com, **br** © Cathy Withers-Clarke - stock.adobe.com
7: tm © bennytrapp - stock.adobe.com, **tr** © Sergey Kolesov - stock.adobe.com, **ml** © Roger de la Harpe - stock.adobe.com, **mr** © davemontreuil - stock.adobe.com, **bl** © Rixie - stock.adobe.com, **br** © byrdyak - stock.adobe.com
8: tl © byrdyak - stock.adobe.com, **mr** © Chris Eason, CC BY-SA 2.0, WC, **bl** BDP, **br** Yathin S Krishnappa, CC BY-SA 3.0, WC
9: t © Nick Dale - stock.adobe.com, **mr** © Clément Bardot, CC BY-SA 4.0, WC, **b** © Photo Designer
10: tr, mr and **bl** BDP, **bml** Brydyak, CC BY-SA 4.0, WC, **bmr** Ltshears, CC BY-SA 3.0, WC, **br** GinaFranchi, CC BY-SA 2.0, WC
11: ml Harvey Barrison, CC BY-SA 2.0, WC, **bl** BDP, **bm** OH, **shrew** Yathin sk, CC BY-SA 3.0, WC, **antlion** Alandmansson CC BY-SA 4.0, WC, **beetle** Chris Burt/Shutterstock.com, **tortoise** karstenggaard from Pixabay, **weaver** Greg Tee, CC BY 2.0, WC
12: l © kostiuchenko - stock.adobe.com, **sunbird** jeanvdmeulen from Pixabay, **pigeon** © Casual-T, **pelican** taviphoto from Pixabay, **eagle-owl** © David - stock.adobe.com, **r** JMK, CC BY-SA 3.0, WC, **b** Uryadnikov Sergey - stock.adobe.com
13: tr, l all three Albert Froneman/IOA, **mr** Yoky, CC By-SA 3.0, WC, **br** © dennisjacobsen - stock.adobe.com
14: tl BDP, **binoculars** © BillionPhotos.com - stock.adobe.com, **note pad** © pixelrobot - stock.adobe.com, **sketches** © drawlab19 - stock.adobe.com, **ml** © Cathy Withers-Clarke - stock.adobe.com, **bl** Alandmansson, CC BY-SA 4.0, WC, **br** © mzphoto11 - stock.adobe.com
15: bird silhouettes © PRH, **eagle** Charles J. Sharp, CC By-SA 4.0, WC, **stork** BDP, **bustard** © Riaan van den Berg - stock.adobe.com, **hornbill** © Tinus Potgieter - stock.adobe.com, **vulture** © EcoView - stock.adobe.com, **owl** © Vaclav - stock.adobe.com
16: tl BDP, **tr** aussieanouk, CC BY-SA 4.0, WC, **ml** © Willem Van Zyl - stock.adobe.com, **mr** BDP, **br** © Mark Kostich - stock.adobe.com
17: tm and **tr** © EcoView - stock.adobe.com, **ml** © Willem Van Zyl - stock.adobe.com, **mr** © geoffsp - stock.adobe.com, **bl** © Kai Co. - stock.adobe.com, **br** © Lady_jane - stock.adobe.com
18: tr © elleonzebon - stock.adobe.com, **mr** JMK, CC BY-SA 3.0, WC, **baobab fruit** DEZALB from Pixabay, **bl** OH, **br** Leo za1, CC BY-SA 3.0, WC
19: tl Gillian Black, **tm** © Rixie - stock.adobe.com, **ml** and **c** BDP, **mrt** SAplants, CC BY-SA 4.0, WC, **mr** © ValenZi - stock.adobe.com, **br** elvirahattingh1 from Pixabay
20: t Harriet S/Shutterstock.com, **ml** Mumpel2000, WC, **mr** "Daniel Fafard (Dreamdan)", CC BY-SA 3.0, WC, **b snake** shaineast/Shutterstock.com, **other silhouettes** © PRH, **br** Mathias Appel, WC
21: t Simon Hurrry on Unsplash.com, **stick insect** © SM, **1.** © Paul Vinten - stock.adobe.com, **2.** © erikzunec - stock.adobe.com, **3.** © Garreth Brown - stock.adobe.com, **4.** © cdrw1973 - stock.adobe.com, **5.** © Martin Mecnarowski - stock.adobe.com, **6.** © suerob - stock.adobe.com, **bl** Derek Keats, CC BY-SA 2.0, WC, **bm** © Ava Peattie - stock.adobe.com, **br** gailhampshire, CC BY-SA 2.0, WC
22: t Rachad sanoussi, CC BY-SA 4.0, WC, **ml** Wendy Dennis/IOA, **mr** Tobie Oosthuizen/Shutterstock.com, **bl** Ben.vandenberg.za, CC BY-SA 4.0, WC, **br** ©Emanuele Biggi/naturepl.com
23: tl OH, **tr** Hari K Patibanda, CC BY 2.0, WC, **m** BDP, **tsessebe** JS/PRH, **all other mammals** SM/© PRH
24: tr Andrew Bannister/IOA, **ml** Michaela Roos from Pixabay, **b** BDP
25: tl and **br** BDP, **tr** Charles J. Shapre, CC BY-SA 4.0, WC
26: tl Anka Eichhoff, **tr** GenesJourney from Pixabay, **ml** Markrosenrosen, CC BY-SA 3.0, WC, **dung** © Peter - stock.adobe.com, **beetle** © allocricetulus - stock.adobe.com, **maze** © Tartila - stock.adobe.com, **bl** © Samantha - stock.adobe.com
27: t all birds PH/© PRH except for **seed-eater** and **insect-eater** © Norman Arlott, **mr** © Nick Dale - stock.adobe.com, **c** © Ava Peattie - stock.adobe.com, **bl** OH
28: tl Jez Bennett/Shutterstock.com, **m** Albie Venter/Shutterstock.com, **bl** Mathias Appel, WC
29: tl Sammy Wong on Unsplash.com, **tr** PH/© PRH, **other illustrations** SM/© PRH, **bl** Andy Reago & Chrissy McClarren, CC BY-SA 2.0
30: Cape fox SM/© PRH, **all other illustrations** JS/PRH, **c** Robart Mwaiteleke/Shutterstock.com, **ml** Frank Vincentz, CC BY-SA 3.0, WC, **b** Andy Morffew, CC BY-SA 2.0, WC
31: tl SasanIAF, CC BY-SA 4.0, WC, **tml** Steven Ward, CC BY-SA 2.0, WC, **tm** and **tmr** Derek Keats, CC BY-SA BY 2.0, WC, **tr** Wayne77, CC BY-SA 3.0, WC, **ml** Luke Verburgt, **bl** SasanIAF, CC BY-SA 4.0, WC, **br** Alandmansson, CC BY-SA 4.0, WC
32: tl Mathias Appel, WC, **bl** Vince Smith, CC BY-SA 2.0, WC, **br** benoit_f/Shutterstock.com
33: tl OH, **tr** © Gerhard - stock.adobe.com, **ml** and **mr** BDP, **bl** Greg Hume, CC BY-SA 3.0, WC, **br** Charles J. Sharp, CC BY-SA 4.0, WC
34: tl BDP, **mr** © Villiers - stock.adobe.com, **bl** © Johncarnemolla - Dreamstime.com, **br** Sergio Pozzetti, WC
35: tl, c breeding red-headed weaver and **non-breeding yellow bishop** Albert Froneman/IOA, **tr** Charles J. Sharp, CC BY-SA 4.0, WC **ml** Jerzy Strzelecki, CC BY-SA 3.0, WC, **ml** Derek Keats, CC BY-SA 2.0, WC, **cr** Lip Kee Yap, CC BY-SA 2.0, WC, **bl** Ryanvanhuyssteen, CC BY-SA 4.0, WC, **br** Jurgens Potgieter/Shutterstock.com
36: tl Colour Library/IOA, **tr** Catherine Merlin on Unsplash.com, **cl** OH, **cml** Derek Keats, CC BY-SA 2.0, WC, **cmr** BDP, **bl** James Wagner, CC BY-SA 4.0, WC, **br** Matt Artz on Unsplash.com
37: tl © phototrip.cz - stock.adobe.com, **tm** Derek Keats, CC BY-SA 2.0, WC, **tr** Montavigus from Pixabay, **ml** © PACO COMO - stock.adobe.com, **c** © Johan Swanepoel/Shutterstock.com, **mr** © Roman Murushkin - Dreamstime.com, **br all** SM/© PRH
38: tr © Alta Oosthuizen - stock.adobe.com, **mr** © Vladimir Wrangel - stock.adobe.com, **b** © Anna - stock.adobe.com
39: tl Derek Keats, CC BY-SA 2.0, **tr** © EcoView - stock.adobe.com, **ml** Olga Ernst & Hp.Baumeler, CC BY-SA 4.0, WC, **mr** Brian Ralphs, CC BY-SA 2.0, WC
40: t © wkbilder - stock.adobe.com, **ml** Didier Descouens, CC BY-SA 4.0, **br** Chantelle Bosch/Shutterstock.com
41: tl © anthony - stock.adobe.com, **tr** © Stefan Scharf - stock.adobe.com, **c** © stuporter - stock.adobe.com, **ml** © Robert Schichtl - stock.adobe.com, **br** BDP
42: t Matt Cramblett on Unsplash.com, **ml** Richard Mortel, CC BY-SA 2.0, WC, **mr** Nigel Dennis/IOA, **b** Ahmed Galal on Unsplash.com, **br** Zamboq, CC BY-SA 2.0, WC
43: tr © Nadine Haase - stock.adobe.com, **wild dog pack** Ian Michler/IOA, **young wild dog** Nigel Dennis/IOA, **lion cubs** © James Heupel/Danita Delimont - stock.adobe.com, **mr** © EtienneOutram - stock.adobe.com, **bl** © ottoduplessis - stock.adobe.com, **br** © PACO COMO - stock.adobe.com
44: tl © Sergey Novikov - stock.adobe.com, **tr** BDP, **ml** Kore, CC BY-SA 3.0, WC, **bl** Frank Vassen, CC BY-SA 2.0, WC, **br** Henrik Hansen on Unsplash.com
45: tl © supasart - stock.adobe.com, **tr** Andy Morffew, CC BY-SA 2.0, WC, **ml** Leonard Hoffmann/IOA, **mr** JMx Images/Shutterstock.com, **bl** © Alta Oosthuizen - stock.adobe.com
46: tm © Lennart - stock.adobe.com, **ml** © Natalia - stock.adobe.com, **mr** © ArtushFoto - stock.adobe.com, **bl** © Cathy Withers-Clarke - stock.adobe.com, **br** Per Harald Olsen, CC BY-SA 3.0
47: tl Mabel Amber from Pixabay, **tr** SABIRAB from Pixabay, **mtr** © Azahara - stock.adobe.com, **mbr** Patrizia08 from Pixabay, **bl** © clickit - stock.adobe.com, **br** Louise Joubert, CC BY-SA 3.0, WC
48: t Bernard Gagnon, CC BY-SA 4,0, WC, **mr** Dror Feitelson, CC BY-SA 3.0, WC, **bl** Art G., CC BY-SA 2.0, WC, **br** Jnissa, CC BY-SA 2.0, WC
49: tr MathKnight and Zachi Evenor, CC BY-SA 4.0, WC, **c** JMx Images/Shutterstock.com, **ml** and **bl** Derek Keats, CC BY-SA 2.0, WC, **bm** and **br** PH/© PRH
50: t six birds all PH/© PRH, **ml** Wonsy, CC BY-SA 4.0, WC, **mc** Dotun55, CC BY-SA 4.0, WC, **mr** Ron Knight, CC BY-SA 2.0, WC, **water monitor** BDP, **bl** Luke Verburgt, **br** Abu Shawka, WC
51: tl Maxime Gilbert on Unsplash.com, **tr** Dave Maguire, CC BY-SA 4.0, WC, **ml** BDP, **mr** Leonard Hoffmann/IOA, **bl** © anatchant - stock.adobe.com, **br** Judy Gallagher, CC BY-SA 2.0, WC
52: tr sirtravelalot/Shutterstock.com, **mtr** Nigel Dennis/IOA, **mbr** PvanDijk from Pixabay, **bl** Yu Miyawaki, CC BY-SA 3.0, WC, **br** Aitor Lamadrid Lopez/Shutterstock.com
53: tr BDP, **ml** Seshadri.K.S, CC BY-SA 3.0, WC, **mc** edie209, CC BY-SA 2.0, WC, **mr** Anka Eichhoff, **br** © Rico Leffanta - Dreamstime.com
54: tl moon Achituv, CC BY-SA 4.0, WC, **leopard** © tcheres - stock.adobe.com, **lion** © Adrian Hillman - stock.adobe.com, **rest of silhouettes** © PRH, **tr** BDP, **ml** PH/© PRH, **c** DanceWithNyanko, CC BY-SA 4.0, WC, **mr** Shayna Take on Unsplash.com, **bl** © slowmotiongli - stock.adobe.com, **br** Laitche, CC BY-SA 4.0, WC
55: tr Vincent Chin on Unsplash.com, **ml** © vchalup - stock.adobe.com, **mr** © Hollygraphic - stock.adobe.com, **bl** Stephen O'Meara, **br** Adrian Eissler, CC BY-SA 3.0, WC
56: t Chris Eason, CC BY 2.0, WC, **mr** JossK/Shutterstock.com, **bl** and **br** BDP, **stars** © YummyBuum - stock.adobe.com
57: tl Alchemist-hp (talk) (www.pse-mendelejew.de), FAL, WC, **tr** David Tomaseti on Unsplash.com, **all other dung images** © Kevin Murray
58: t Used with permission from !Xaus Lodge. © Charles O'Leary, **all mammals** SM/© PRH, **b** © Jeffrey Banke - stock.adobe.com
59: all mammals SM/© PRH, **tr** PH/© PRH, **mrt** © saodaengl - stock.adobe.com, **mrb** Amada44, CC BY-SA 4.0, WC, **brt** © Valdimir Wrangel - stock.adobe.com, **br** © den123 - stock.adobe.com
60: tl and **c** SM/© PRH, **br** Lanz von Hörsten/IOA
61: tl © JethroT, **quills** © SM, **tl** &Beyond www.andBeyond.com, **tr** © marioforsos - stock.adobe.com, **mr** JMK, CC BY-SA 4.0, WC, **bl** © Darrel - stock.adobe.com, **br** © Nabiru - stock.adobe.com

64